The Art of LANDSCAPE KNITTING

BEGINNER KNITTING PATTERNS FOR UNIQUE BLANKETS

ANNE LE BROCQ

DAVID & CHARLES

www.davidandcharles.com

Contents

Square Patterns

Introduction

This book aims to be an antidote to the modern pace of living, allowing you to take a moment to slow down, to reconnect with and notice the small details of nature. When you go for a walk with a small child, you have to stop frequently to examine something – be it a bug, a flower, or to poke something with a stick. The contrast with our busy adult lives is stark; we often get lost in the big things and don't take the time to engage in the mindful practice of noticing the small things.

This project has grown out of a long-term habit of taking 'pattern pictures' – taking photographs of repeating patterns in nature. I started to knit blankets as a way of occupying a busy and restless mind, finding books with patterns of squares with various abstract textures. The idea started to germinate of making textured squares inspired by patterns in the landscape, and building them into 'blanketscapes'. The final inspiration was found on a 6-week solo motorcycle trip up the west coast of Scotland. I bought yarn as I went, knitted squares and posted them home, ready to turn into a blanket when I returned. I bought a multicolour ball from a wool shop in Stornoway on the Isle of Lewis, which knitted up squares just like a stormy Hebridean beach scene. So, I started to think about a full-size blanket made of textured squares inspired by the landscape, using the colours of the Stornoway squares as the basis.

I spent many happy days on the beaches around my home in Devon, thinking about the patterns I came across. Then I incorporated them into simple square patterns to build the blanketscapes from. The project gave me a reason to get out and about, and also something to occupy me back at home. It also gave me an item that evoked the various trips I had been on to gain the inspiration. I then decided to branch out (if you'll excuse the pun) into forest patterns, which took me to forests and woods I would never have otherwise been to. Before this project I didn't know a great deal about tree species, but now I am able to identify some of the more common ones!

Connecting with the environment gives us an awareness of the incredible world we live in and we should do what we can to protect it. Spending time in nature is good for physical and mental wellbeing, engaging all the senses. You could be standing on a beach feeling the sun on your face and listening to the waves, or in a forest hearing the squelch of your boots in the mud, feeling the texture of a tree trunk while trying to keep your footing. Being out in all weathers across the seasons, you notice how the same part of the world can look very different, and inspire different emotions. I hope the textures in this book evoke all these feelings and, through building your own blanketscape inspired by a place that means a lot to you, you will create something that will transport you back to that place – whilst also keeping you warm!

How to Use this Book

This book provides 50 square patterns representing various textures and patterns in the landscape. I wanted the patterns to be fairly simple and easy to follow, both for beginners to start on their knitting journey, or for those who, like me, tend to knit with the television on at the same time! The square patterns are divided into groups for different landscapes, or parts of the landscape, but you can mix and match the squares as you like to create your own blanketscape. Seven example blankets are included, demonstrating a variety of landscapes, colours and approaches.

The square patterns are designed to repeat horizontally and vertically so they can be used to build any size of blanket. Any squares with 'Combined' in the title will only repeat horizontally, however; these combined squares are provided for making the smallest size of baby blanket, while still incorporating a variety of textures. All squares (apart from the three Pebbly Beach squares) use 36 stitches, so the patterns are consistent as you work your way up the landscape. Most are 48 rows in height, apart from the Many Footprints square, though depending on the nature of the texture the different squares often come out different ratios, especially before blocking. I used 3.75mm (US size 5) needles for the sample squares in the pattern directory, and mostly Stylecraft Special DK, so they measure 17 x 17cm (6¾ x 6¾in).

The patterns are mainly made with only knits and purls, reversing the stitches to make the pattern pop out. With a horizonal pattern such as Sand Waves, the wrong-side stocking (stockinette) stitch is the side that is raised (as you would expect from garter stitch), so the wrong side provides the texture. For a vertical pattern, such as Beech Tree Trunks it is the right side stocking (stockinette) stitch that is raised (as you would expect from a rib stitch), so the patterns are made with the right side providing the texture.

Following the charts

The charts show how to create the textures, with each square equal to one stitch, and an 'x' denoting when you need to knit on a wrong-side row and purl on a right-side row. Read the charts from the bottom upward; right-side rows are white and read from right to left, whereas wrong-side rows are grey and read from left to right. The numbers in some squares show how many times you need to work the same stitch in a block of stitches before you change to the other. They are only given in the middle of groups of more than three of the same stitch, so where there is a number shown you should work the same stitch as indicated on either side, and they are only on the first repeat where the pattern repeats itself vertically. The numbers are different on the three Pebble patterns – here the number plus arrow shows how many rows below you should work that stitch (see Tips & Techniques: Drop Stitch). Stocking (stockinette) stitch rows begin with a knit row unless otherwise stated. The written instructions provide an alternative for those who prefer them to following a chart.

Note

Some of the square patterns contain reverse-side stocking stitches in the first row. If you are making a blanket in one piece using these squares, and using different colours for each square pattern element, you will get a mixed colour stitch. It will look neater if you work a plain knit row in the new colour for the first row of each square pattern, rather than the first pattern row (see picture). If you are working with a gradient yarn, or are holding different colour yarns together (as with the Deciduous Woodland blanket), this isn't necessary as there will not be a hard colour change.

The blankets

The blankets can be made either from individual squares seamed together, or they can be made in one piece. To make in one piece, simply place stitch markers at the start and end of each square pattern, then repeat it the desired number of times across the row. I tend to use little loops of yarn for stitch markers rather than rigid markers when I'm using thin yarn for the blanket, otherwise it can leave a mark in the knitting. The Sunny Beach blanket shows how the blankets can be made both ways, demonstrating the difference in the two approaches. The rest of the example blanket patterns are a mix of the two approaches. If the squares are made individually, some are finished with an extra right-side row to make the pattern more symmetrical. A border can be added afterwards by picking up and knitting stitches around the edges. Squares knitted individually will definitely need blocking, because they tend to get a bit scrunchy. However, even a blanket made in one piece will also benefit from blocking at the end of the make to help the stitches sit more evenly.

The example blankets demonstrate how different approaches to the colour of the blanket can be taken. The Snowy Mountain blanket uses a single colour throughout, whereas all the others use a variety of colour palettes found in each of the landscapes, either as a gradient or with hard colour horizons.

Tools & Materials

The square patterns included in the book are designed to be flexible enough for any yarn type, weight or colour to be utilised to make any size, shape or weight of blanket; ranging from a lightweight summer baby blanket to a heavyweight bedspread. The following sections outline the types of yarn you could use, the colour schemes you could incorporate and the needles best suited to each type of project.

CHOICE OF YARN

The example blankets in the book aim to demonstrate the range of fibre types, weights and colours you could use in your blanketscape. The options are transferable across all landscape types, so you can make the landscape that inspires you, to your own design specifications. The choice of yarn depends on the purpose of the blanket, your personal preference and budget. A range of fibres are used here, with mostly mixed yarns, including acrylic, cotton, bamboo, wool and recycled yarn. Each yarn has its pros and cons, in terms of both usability and environmental impact. Life is full of compromises but, whatever your choice, the important factor is that the item is used and treasured for a long time. This is all the more likely for a blanket made with love (and hopefully not too much blood, sweat and tears), rather than a cheap, mass-manufactured item.

Acrylic yarn

A small blanket for a baby needs a soft yarn that is easily washable, so an acrylic yarn is often a go-to choice. It is also relatively low priced and often comes with an extensive range of colours to choose from for your landscape. The downside of acrylic yarn, however, is that is sheds a lot of microfibres into the environment when washed.

Cotton and bamboo yarn

Natural yarns, such as cotton or bamboo, are equally soft and a good choice for a baby blanket but do require a bit more care when washing. Cotton has a good drape and is smooth to knit with; the 4-ply (sportweight) cotton held double for the Deciduous Woodland blanket creates a super-warm and heavy blanket. The environmental impact of growing cotton is also not negligible however, because it requires a large amount of water and fertiliser for growth. Bamboo is fast growing and requires less resources than cotton to grow, so has potentially the least environmental impact. However, it still needs to be grown in a sustainable way, without creating a commercial mono-culture.

Wool yarn

Despite some types being itchy, wool can still be a good choice for a baby blanket if chosen carefully. Merino wool, for example, is super-soft, warm and washable. Hand-dyed yarns are now widely available that utilise local sources of wool, and provide a range of beautiful colour palettes. For a general-use blanket, wool is warm and hard-wearing. Wool has a lot of benefits, but it is not without its environmental impact, with sheep farming causing land-use change and greenhouse gas emissions. You also have to be careful of those pesky moths!

Recycled yarn

Finally, there are more recycled yarns becoming available, which provide a more sustainable option – but still retain the pros and cons of the original fibre of course.

Yarn weight conversion chart

UK	US
4-ply	Sportweight
DK	Light worsted
Aran	Worsted
Chunky	Bulky

Some yarns do vary from the weight given on the ball band and the type of yarn also affects the length of yarn in a ball. It is always a good idea to work up a tension (gauge) swatch in your chosen yarn before beginning your blanketscape.

CHOICE OF COLOUR

There's a range of ways in which colour can be used to represent the landscape – this is when the blanket stops becoming something to keep you warm, but starts to turn into a personalised work of art! The colours you choose will reflect your artistic preference, either light tonal colours with a soft gradient, or brighter colours creating harder horizons. It also depends on who you are making the blanket for; a child may prefer brighter colours, compared to a more refined palette for an adult's blanket. Your budget is also a factor here, since knitting a small blanket in a single colour minimises the left-over yarn at the end of a project. Yarn cakes with a built in gradient provide a ready-made colour scheme that gradually changes, or you can create your own gradients by holding the yarn double and swapping the colours in and out. Some landscapes, like beaches, do have sharper colour horizons, so work well with a hard change of colour. This can be done when making a blanket in one piece as well as in squares, changing the yarn colour when you start a new square pattern, either with a join or leaving yarn ends to be sewn into the border when you have finished.

CHOICE OF NEEDLES

If you are making a blanket out of individual squares, then straight single-pointed needles can be used. I use super-short children's needles when I'm on my travels, so they don't get bent and I'm less likely to annoy the person in the seat next to me by poking them! For blankets made in one piece then circular needles work best, the longer the better to avoid too much bunching of the stitches. My tension is generally quite loose, so I often have to use a smaller needle size than suggested on a ball band. If you knit tightly, then knitting a tension square is important to reproduce the colour changes and utitlize the appropriate amount of yarn.

Needle size conversion chart

UK	US
2mm	0
2.25mm	1
2.5mm	–
2.75mm	2
3mm	–
3.25mm	3
3.5mm	4
3.75mm	5
4mm	6
4.5mm	7
5mm	8
5.5mm	9
6mm	10

Terrain

We will start at the bottom of the blanket, looking down at our feet and thinking about the terrain we might move over in the landscape. **Many Footprints** represents the pattern of many feet moving over a soft surface, leaving an imprint. Treading over soft sand on the beach is quiet, whereas the squelchy-ness of a muddy footpath, or the crunchiness of snow underfoot is a sound evocative of the time of year. The footprints in the landscape show us 'desire lines' - the easiest path to a destination, perhaps up through the dunes by the beach, or around a muddy puddle. On sand that has been freshly revealed by a receding tide, or on a fresh fall of snow, there might be isolated sets of footprints crossing the landscape as represented in **Few Footprints**. **Combined Footprints** blends these two patterns into a single square for smaller blanket patterns.

There may instead be beautiful green grass, either well-kept or a bit clumpy where you have to watch your step to avoid turning an ankle. **Grass** is a simple pattern to represent the vertical lines of well-kept grass, the length of which could be tailored as you wish. In the springtime bluebells might appear in the grass beneath deciduous woodland, creating a stunning carpet of blue. They take advantage of the early spring light before the deciduous trees regain their leaves. Bluebells have a rich folklore backstory – telling us that these are fairy bells calling the fairies to a gathering. But don't listen too carefully as you knit **Bluebells**, as the outlook for a human that hears the bells is apparently not good...

Turbulent water, created by a river flowing around rocks, is represented by **Troubled Water**, a phrase made famous by a certain Simon and Garfunkel song (the one with the bridge). This kind of river is a good metaphor for life: it flows inexorably to its destination, with some turbulence along the way. But at high water flow levels, sometimes you just have to get the kayak out and make the best of it.

01 / MANY FOOTPRINTS

One-piece blanket

Repeat each row across the blanket as many times as required for the size you are making.

*Row 1: K5, p8, k10, p8, k5.
Row 2: P4, k2, p6, k2, p8, k2, p6, k2, p4.
Row 3: K3, p2, k8, p2, k6, p2, k8, p2, k3.
Row 4: K4, p10, k8, p10, k4.
Row 5: P3, k12, p6, k12, p3.
Row 6: K4, p10, k8, p10, k4.
Row 7: K3, p2, k8, p2, k6, p2, k8, p2, k3.
Row 8: P4, k2, p6, k2, p8, k2, p6, k2, p4.
Row 9: K5, p8, k10, p8, k5.
Row 10: P6, k6, p12, k6, p6**
Rows 11 to 50: Rep Rows 1 to 10 four times more.

Individual squares

Cast on 36 sts.

Work from * to **.

Rows 11 to 49: Rep Rows 1 to 10 three times more, then Rows 1 to 9 once more.

Cast (bind) off purlwise.

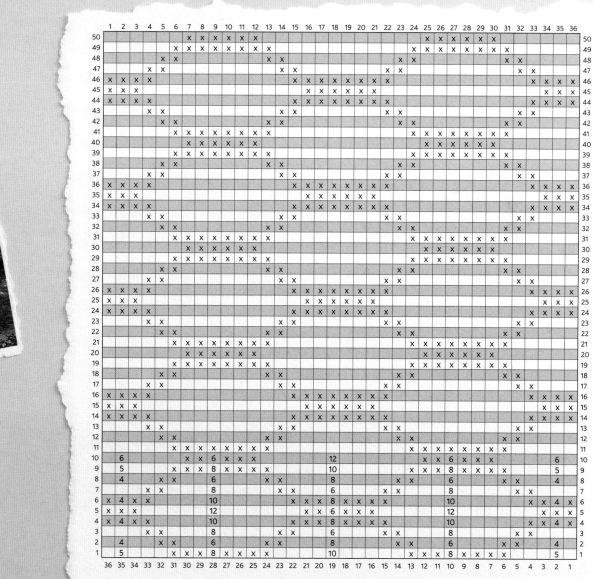

Footprints are usually transient features in the landscape, washed away by the tide or melting with the snow. Sometimes they stay around for a while, as in mud that dries quickly at the changing of the seasons. The footprints here are abstract in shape, to follow the pattern of the Many Footprints square for consistency.

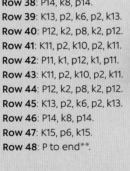

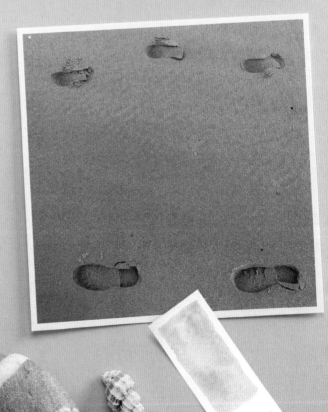

One-piece blanket

Repeat each row across the blanket as many times as required for the size you are making.

*Row 1: K to end.
Row 2: P24, k6, p6.
Row 3: K5, p8, k23.
Row 4: P22, k2, p6, k2, p4.
Row 5: K3, p2, k8, p2, k21.
Row 6: P20, k2, p10, k2, p2.
Row 7: K2, p1, k12, p1, k20.
Row 8: P20, k2, p10, k2, p2.
Row 9: K3, p2, k8, p2, k21.
Row 10: P22, k2, p6, k2, p4.
Row 11: K5, p8, k23.
Row 12: P6, k6, p12, k6, p6.
Row 13: K23, p8, k5.
Row 14: P4, k2, p6, k2, p22.
Row 15: K21, p2, k8, p2, k3.
Row 16: P2, k2, p10, k2, p20.
Row 17: K20, p1, k12, p1, k2.
Row 18: P2, k2, p10, k2, p20.
Row 19: K21, p2, k8, p2, k3.
Row 20: P4, k2, p6, k2, p22.
Row 21: K23, p8, k5.
Row 22: P6, k6, p24.
Rows 23 to 26: St st four rows.
Row 27: P3, k30, p3.
Row 28: K4, p28, k4.
Row 29: K3, p2, k26, p2, k3.
Row 30: P4, k2, p24, k2, p4.
Row 31: K5, p2, k22, p2, k5.
Row 32: P6, k1, p22, k1, p6.
Row 33: K5, p2, k22, p2, k5.
Row 34: P4, k2, p24, k2, p4.

Row 35: K3, p2, k26, p2, k3.
Row 36: K4, k28, k4.
Row 37: P3, k12, p6, k12, p3.
Row 38: P14, k8, p14.
Row 39: K13, p2, k6, p2, k13.
Row 40: P12, k2, p8, k2, p12.
Row 41: K11, p2, k10, p2, k11.
Row 42: P11, k1, p12, k1, p11.
Row 43: K11, p2, k10, p2, k11.
Row 44: P12, k2, p8, k2, p12.
Row 45: K13, p2, k6, p2, k13.
Row 46: P14, k8, p14.
Row 47: K15, p6, k15.
Row 48: P to end**.

Individual squares

Cast on 36 sts.

Work from * to **.

Cast (bind) off.

	1	2	3	4	5	6	7	8	9	10	11	12	13	14	15	16	17	18	19	20	21	22	23	24	25	26	27	28	29	30	31	32	33	34	35	36	
48																																					48
47									15							x	x	6	x	x	x							15									47
46									14						x	x	x	8	x	x	x	x	x					14									46
45									13					x	x			6					x	x				13									45
44									12				x	x				8						x	x			12									44
43									11			x	x					10							x	x		11									43
42									11			x						12								x		11									42
41									11			x	x					10							x	x		11									41
40									12				x	x				8						x	x			12									40
39									13					x	x			6					x	x				13									39
38									14						x	x	x	8	x	x	x	x						14									38
37	x	x	x						12							x	x	6	x	x	x							12						x	x	x	37
36	x	4	x	x														28															x	x	4	x	36
35			x	x														26													x	x					35
34		4			x	x												24												x	x			4			34
33		5					x	x										22											x	x					5		33
32		6						x										22											x						6		32
31		5					x	x										22											x	x					5		31
30		4			x	x												24												x	x			4			30
29			x	x														26													x	x					29
28	x	4	x	x														28															x	4	x	x	28
27	x	x	x															30																x	x	x	27
26																																					26
25																																					25
24																																					24
23																																					23
22		6						x	x	6	x	x	x							24																	22
21		5					x	x	x	8	x	x	x	x	x					23																	21
20		4				x	x			6			x	x						22																	20
19				x	x					8				x	x					21																	19
18			x	x						10					x	x				20																	18
17			x							12						x				20																	17
16			x	x						10					x	x				20																	16
15				x	x					8				x	x					21																	15
14		4				x	x			6			x	x						22																	14
13		5					x	x	x	8	x	x	x	x						23																	13
12		6						x	x	6	x	x	x							12			x	x	6	x	x	x						6			12
11									23															x	x	x	8	x	x	x	x				5		11
10									22																x	x	6				x	x			4		10
9									21																	x	x	8				x	x				9
8									20																x	x		10			x	x					8
7									20																	x		12				x					7
6									20																x	x		10			x	x					6
5									21																	x	x	8		x	x						5
4									22																	x	x	6		x	x			4			4
3									23																x	x	x	8	x	x	x				5		3
2									24																x	x	6	x	x	x				6			2
1																																					1
	36	35	34	33	32	31	30	29	28	27	26	25	24	23	22	21	20	19	18	17	16	15	14	13	12	11	10	9	8	7	6	5	4	3	2	1	

One-piece blanket

Repeat each row across the blanket as many times as required for the size you are making.

*Row 1: P3, k12, p6, k12, p3.
Row 2: K4, p10, k8, p10, k4.
Row 3: K3, p2, k8, p2, k6, p2, k8, p2, k3.
Row 4: P4, k2, p6, k2, p8, k2, p6, k2, p4.
Row 5: K5, p8, k10, p8, k5.
Row 6: P6, k6, p12, k6, p6.
Row 7: K5, p8, k10, p8, k5.
Row 8: P4, k2, p6, k2, p8, k2, p6, k2, p4.
Row 9: K3, p2, k8, p2, k6, p2, k8, p2, k3.
Row 10: K4, p10, k8, p10, k4.
Rows 11 to 20: Rep Rows 1 to 10.
Row 21: P3, k12, p6, k12, p3.
Row 22: P2, k2, p10, k2, p20.
Row 23: K21, p2, k8, p2, k3.
Row 24: P4, k2, p6, k2, p22.
Row 25: K23, p8, k5.
Row 26: P6, k6, p12, k6, p6.
Row 27: K5, p8, k23.
Row 28: P22, k2, p6, k2, p4.
Row 29: K3, p2, k8, p2, k21.
Row 30: P20, k2, p10, k2, p2.
Row 31: K2, p1, k12, p1, k20.
Row 32: P20, k2, p10, k2, p2.
Row 33: K3, p2, k8, p2, k21.

Row 34: P22, k2, p6, k2, p4.
Row 35: K5, p8, k23.
Row 36: P6, k6, p12, k6, p6.
Row 37: K23, p8, k5.
Row 38: P4, k2, p6, k2, p22.
Row 39: K21, p2, k8, p2, k3.
Row 40: P2, k2, p10, k2, p20.
Row 41: K20, p1, k12, p1, k2.
Row 42: P2, k2, p10, k2, p20.
Row 43: K21, p2, k8, p2, k3.
Row 44: P4, k2, p6, k2, p22.
Row 45: K23, p8, k5.
Row 46: P6, k6, p24.
Rows 47 and 48: St st two rows**.

Individual squares

Cast on 36 sts.
Work from * to **.
Cast (bind) off.

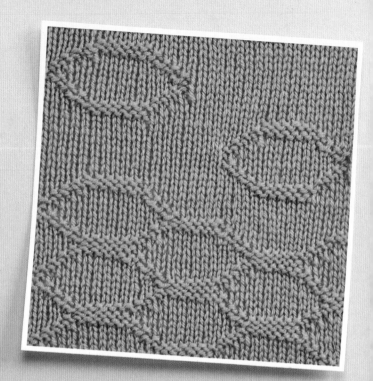

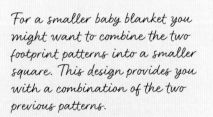

For a smaller baby blanket you might want to combine the two footprint patterns into a smaller square. This design provides you with a combination of the two previous patterns.

	1	2	3	4	5	6	7	8	9	10	11	12	13	14	15	16	17	18	19	20	21	22	23	24	25	26	27	28	29	30	31	32	33	34	35	36	
48																																					48
47																																					47
46		6					x	x	x	6	x	x																							24		46
45		5				x	x	x	x	8	x	x	x																						23		45
44		4			x	x				6				x	x																				22		44
43			x	x						8				x	x																				21		43
42		x	x							10					x	x																			20		42
41		x								12					x																				20		41
40		x	x							10					x	x																			20		40
39			x	x						8				x	x																				21		39
38		4			x	x				6				x	x																				22		38
37		5				x	x	x	x	8	x	x	x																						23		37
36		6					x	x	x	6	x	x							12					x	x	x		6	x	x					6		36
35		23																					x	x	x	x		8	x	x	x				5		35
34		22																				x	x					6			x	x			4		34
33		21																					x	x				8				x	x				33
32		20																				x	x					10					x	x			32
31		20																				x						12						x			31
30		20																				x	x					10					x	x			30
29		21																					x	x				8				x	x				29
28		22																				x	x					6			x	x			4		28
27		23																					x	x	x	x		8	x	x	x				5		27
26		6					x	x	x	6	x	x							12					x	x	x		6	x	x					6		26
25		5				x	x	x	x	8	x	x	x															23									25
24		4			x	x				6				x	x													22									24
23			x	x						8				x	x													21									23
22		x	x							10					x	x												20									22
21	x	x	x							12					x	x	x	6	x	x								12					x	x	x	x	21
20	x	4	x	x						10					x	x	x	x	8	x	x	x						10					x	x	4	x	20
19			x	x						8				x	x				6		x	x						8				x	x				19
18		4			x	x				6				x	x				8				x	x				6			x	x			4		18
17		5				x	x	x	x	8	x	x	x						10					x	x	x		8	x	x	x				5		17
16		6					x	x	x	6	x	x							12					x	x	x		6	x	x					6		16
15		5				x	x	x	x	8	x	x	x						10					x	x	x		8	x	x	x				5		15
14		4			x	x				6				x	x				8				x	x				6			x	x			4		14
13			x	x						8				x	x				6		x	x						8				x	x				13
12		4	x	x						10					x	x	x	x	8	x	x	x						10					x	x	4	x	12
11	x	x	x							12					x	x	x	6	x	x								12						x	x	x	11
10	x	4	x	x						10					x	x	x	x	8	x	x	x						10					x	x	4	x	10
9			x	x						8				x	x				6		x	x						8				x	x				9
8		4			x	x				6				x	x				8				x	x				6			x	x			4		8
7		5				x	x	x	x	8	x	x	x						10					x	x	x		8	x	x	x				5		7
6		6					x	x	x	6	x	x							12					x	x	x		6	x	x					6		6
5		5				x	x	x	x	8	x	x	x						10					x	x	x		8	x	x	x				5		5
4		4			x	x				6				x	x				8				x	x				6			x	x			4		4
3			x	x						8				x	x				6		x	x						8				x	x				3
2	x	4	x	x						10					x	x	x	x	8	x	x	x						10					x	x	4	x	2
1	x	x	x							12					x	x	x	6	x	x								12						x	x	x	1
	36	35	34	33	32	31	30	29	28	27	26	25	24	23	22	21	20	19	18	17	16	15	14	13	12	11	10	9	8	7	6	5	4	3	2	1	

One-piece blanket

Repeat each row across the blanket as many times as required for the size you are making. Note: if you have a hard colour change against the previous square, knit across Row 1 for a neater join, instead of working the pattern row.

*Row 1: [P1, k1] 18 times.
Rows 2 to 4: Rep Row 1 three times more.
Row 5: [K1, p1] 18 times.

Rows 6 to 8: Rep Row 5 three times more.
Rows 9 to 48: Rep Rows 1 to 8 five times more**.

Individual squares

Cast on 36 sts.
Work from * to **.
Cast (bind) off.

05 / BLUEBELLS

One-piece blanket

Repeat each row across the blanket as many times as required for the size you are making. Note: if you have a hard colour change against the previous square, knit across Row 1 for a neater join, instead of working the pattern row.

*Row 1: P4, [k1, p8] three times, k1, p4.
Row 2: K2, [p5, k4] three times, p5, k2.
Row 3: P2, [k5, p4] three times, k5, p2.
Row 4: K3, [p3, k6] three times, p3, k3.
Row 5: P3, [k3, p6] three times, k3, p3.
Rows 6 to 9: Rep Rows 4 and 5 twice more.
Row 10: K4, [p1, k8] three times, p1, k4.

Row 11: P4, [k1, p8] three times, k1, p4.
Row 12: K4, [p1, k8] three times, p1, k4.
Row 13: [P8, k1] four times.
Row 14: P3, [k4, p5] three times, k4, p2.
Row 15: K2, [p4, k5] three times, p4, k3.
Row 16: P2, [k6, p3] three times, k6, p1.
Row 17: K1, [p6, k3] three times, p6, k2.
Rows 18 to 21: Rep Rows 16 and 17 twice more.
Row 22: [P1, k8] four times.
Row 23: [P8, k1] four times.
Row 24: [P1, k8] four times.
Rows 25 to 48: Rep Rows 1 to 24**.

Individual squares

Cast on 36 sts.
Work from * to **.
Cast (bind) off.

06 / TROUBLED WATER

The troubled water in this square is created by large rocks in the river, which force the water to flow around them making turbulence downstream of the obstacle. I have attempted to capture the dynamism of the water using a small amount of moss (seed) stitch, which emphasises the frothy water around the rocks.

One-piece blanket

Repeat each row across the blanket as many times as required for the size you are making.

*Rows 1 and 2: St st two rows.
Row 3: K16, [p1, k1] five times, p1, k9.
Row 4: P6, [k1, p1] nine times, k1, p11.
Row 5: K8, [p1, k1] 11 times, p1, k5.
Row 6: P4, k1, p1, k7, [p1, k1] six times, p11.
Row 7: K12, [p1, k1] five times, p9, k5.
Row 8: P6, k9, [p1, k1] three times, p15.
Row 9: K18, [p1, k1] twice, p8, k6.
Row 10: P7, k6, p23.
Row 11: K24, p4, k8.
Row 12 to 14: St st three rows (starting with a p row).
Row 15: K10, [p1, k1] five times, p1, k15.
Row 16: P12, [k1, p1] nine times, k1, p5.
Row 17: K2, [p1, k1] 11 times, p1, k11.

Row 18: P10, k1, p1, k7, [p1, k1] six times, p5.
Row 19: K6, [p1, k1] five times, p9, k11.
Row 20: P12, k9, [p1, k1] three times, p9.
Row 21: K12, [p1, k1] twice, p8, k12.
Row 22: P13, k6, p17.
Row 23: K18, p4, k14.
Row 24: P to end.
Rows 25 to 48: Rep Rows 1 to 24**.

Individual squares

Cast on 36 sts.

Work from * to **.

Cast (bind) off purlwise.

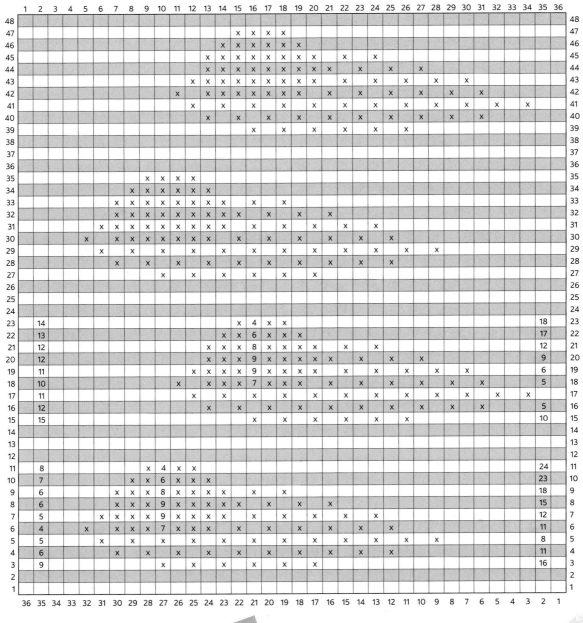

Beach

Beaches provide a variety of characteristic patterns for a beachscape blanket. The dry sand above the tideline may be criss-crossed by the footprints of many people, as with Many Footprints, Few Footprints and Combined Footprints in the Terrain section. Moving beyond the tideline there are different patterns to be found in wet sand, disturbed only by the odd dog and their human.

Sand waves, or ripples, found in some areas of wet sand are particularly fascinating – represented by **Sand Waves**. The ripples form due to the turbulent movement of the water above; they are lost when the tide goes out but protected in pools where water remains until it drains away into the sand. Small pebbles and other objects create diagonal repeating patterns on the sand as the water retreats with the tide. Adding small 'pebbles' of reverse stocking stitch to **Pebbly Sand** recreates these diagonal lines. **Combined Wet Sand** blends the two wet sand patterns into a single square.

A pebbly beach presents a very different experience to a sandy one, but on a stormy day it provides a multi-sensory experience – with the noise of breaking waves crashing onto the pebbles, and a deafening roar as pebbles are drawn towards the sea by the retreating wave. Three sizes of pebble squares are provided, used either to represent sorting of the pebbles, or perspective as viewed from the beach.

The sight and sounds of repetitive waves breaking onto a beach are very therapeutic. The waves may have formed due to local winds, or travelled a great distance as a swell before crashing onto the shore. The breaking part of the wave gradually spreads along the wave as it approaches the shore, so two sizes of breaking waves are provided: **Large Breaking Waves** and **Small Breaking Waves**. Pebbly Beach shows how these squares can be used together. For a smaller blanket the two patterns are used in **Combined Breaking Waves**.

Palm tree patterns add a tropical feel to your beach blanket. Palm trunks vary in texture – **Palm Tree Trunks** represents a date palm, which is rough in comparison to others. Palm fronds grow out from the crown of the tree, so **Palm Tree Fronds** is a complex pattern to reproduce the texture of pinnate (feather-leaved) fronds of a date or coconut palm.

Sand ripples form different patterns of varying sizes.

One-piece blanket

Repeat each row across the blanket as many times as required for the size you are making.

*Row 1: K to end.
Row 2: K4, p10, k8, p10, k4.
Row 3: P6, k6, p12, k6, p6.
Row 4: K to end.
Row 5: K3, p12, k6, p12, k3.
Row 6: P5, k8, p10, k8, p5.
Rows 7 to 48: Rep Rows 1 to 6 seven times more******.

Individual squares

Cast on 36 sts.

Work from * to **.

Row 49: K to end.
Cast (bind) off purlwise.

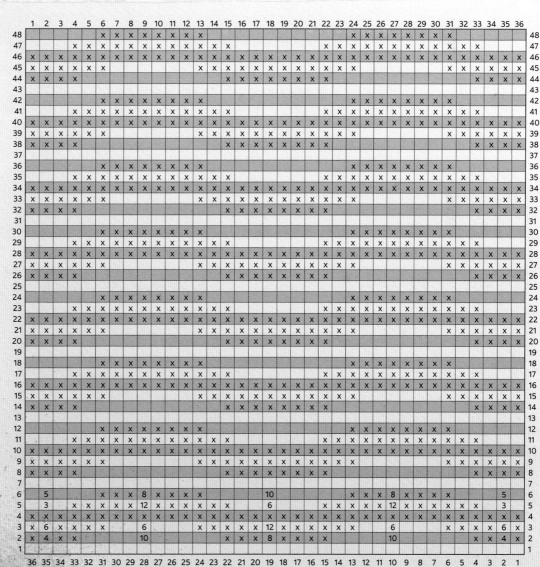

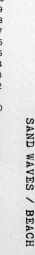

08 / PEBBLY SAND

One-piece blanket

Repeat each row across the blanket as many times as required for the size you are making.

*Row 1: K to end.
Row 2: P8, [k2, p10] twice, k2, p2.
Row 3: K2, [p2, k10] twice, p2, k8.
Rows 4 to 6: St st three rows (starting with a p row).
Row 7: K8, [p2, k10] twice, p2, k2.
Row 8: P2, [k2, p10] twice, k2, p8.
Rows 9 to 11: St st three rows.
Rows 12 to 48: Rep Rows 2 to 11 three times more, then Rows 2 to 8 once more**

Individual squares

Cast on 36 sts.

Work from * to **.

Row 49: K to end.

Cast (bind) off purlwise.

Row	1	2	3	4	5	6	7	8	9	10	11	12	13	14	15	16	17	18	19	20	21	22	23	24	25	26	27	28	29	30	31	32	33	34	35	36
48			x	x											x	x											x	x								
47			x	x											x	x											x	x								
46																																				
45																																				
44																																				
43									x	x											x	x											x	x		
42									x	x											x	x											x	x		
41																																				
40																																				
39																																				
38			x	x											x	x											x	x								
37			x	x											x	x											x	x								
36																																				
35																																				
34																																				
33									x	x											x	x											x	x		
32									x	x											x	x											x	x		
31																																				
30																																				
29																																				
28			x	x											x	x											x	x								
27			x	x											x	x											x	x								
26																																				
25																																				
24																																				
23									x	x											x	x											x	x		
22									x	x											x	x											x	x		
21																																				
20																																				
19																																				
18			x	x											x	x											x	x								
17			x	x											x	x											x	x								
16																																				
15																																				
14																																				
13									x	x											x	x											x	x		
12									x	x											x	x											x	x		
11																																				
10																																				
9																																				
8			x	x					10						x	x					10						x	x					8			
7			x	x					10						x	x					10						x	x					8			
6																																				
5																																				
4																																				
3				8					x	x					10						x	x					10						x	x		
2				8					x	x					10						x	x					10						x	x		
1																																				

| 36 | 35 | 34 | 33 | 32 | 31 | 30 | 29 | 28 | 27 | 26 | 25 | 24 | 23 | 22 | 21 | 20 | 19 | 18 | 17 | 16 | 15 | 14 | 13 | 12 | 11 | 10 | 9 | 8 | 7 | 6 | 5 | 4 | 3 | 2 | 1 |

09 / COMBINED WET SAND

One-piece blanket

Repeat each row across the blanket as many times as required for the size you are making.

*Row 1: K to end.
Row 2: P8, [k2, p10] twice, k2, p2.
Row 3: K2, [p2, k10] twice, p2, k8.
Rows 4 to 6: St st three rows (starting with a p row).
Row 7: K8, [p2, k10] twice, p2, k2.
Row 8: P2, [k2, p10] twice, k2, p8.
Rows 9 and 10: St st two rows.
Rows 11 to 20: Rep Rows 1 to 10.
Rows 21 to 25: Rep Rows 1 to 5.
Row 26: K4, p10, k8, p10, k4.

Row 27: P6, k6, p12, k6, p6.
Row 28: K to end.
Row 29: K3, p12, k6, p12, k3.
Row 30: P5, k8, p10, k8, p5.
Row 31: K to end.
Rows 32 to 48: Rep Rows 26 to 31 twice more, then Rows 26 to 30 once more ******.

Individual squares

Cast on 36 sts.

Work from * to **.

Row 49: K to end.
Cast (bind) off purlwise.

10 / LARGE PEBBLES

Pattern

Cast on 32 sts.

Rows 1 to 7: St st seven rows (starting with a p row).

Row 8: K6, [k6b, k7] three times, k6b, k1.

Rows 9 to 17: St st nine rows (starting with a p row).

Row 18: K2, [k6b, k7] three times, k6b, k5.

Rows 19 to 27: St st nine rows (starting with a p row).

Rows 28 to 47: Rep Rows 8 to 27 once more.

Rows 48 to 58: Rep Rows 8 to 18 once more.

Row 59: P to end.

Cast (bind) off.

A pebbly beach is made up of smooth flat pebbles with their edges worn by years of erosion from the sea, perfect for practising your skimming technique. A modified bubble stitch, with dropped stitches, is used here to represent the round pebbles of differing sizes.

MEDIUM PEBBLES

Pattern

Cast on 30 sts.

Rows 1 to 5: St st five rows (starting with a p row).
Row 6: K4, [k5b, k5] four times, k5b, k1.
Rows 7 to 13: St st seven rows (starting with a p row).
Row 14: K1, [k5b, k5] four times, k4.
Rows 15 to 21: St st seven rows (starting with a purl row).
Rows 22 to 53: Rep Rows 6 to 21 twice more.
Rows 54 to 62: Rep Rows 6 to 14 once more.
Row 63: P to end.
Cast (bind) off.

You can find interesting shapes and patterns on a pebbly beach.

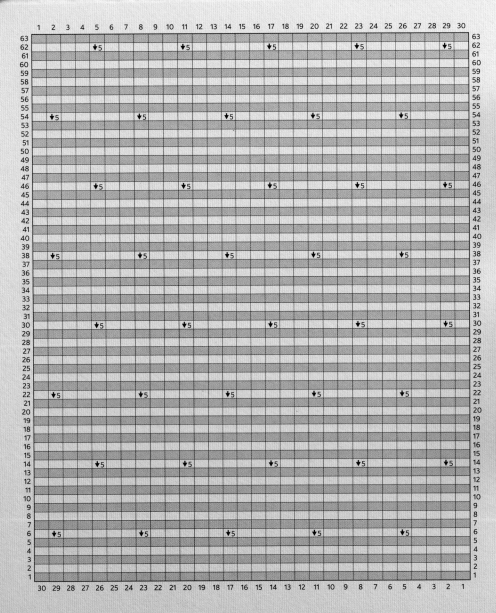

12 / SMALL PEBBLES

Pattern

Cast on 29 sts.

Rows 1 to 5: St st five rows (starting with a p row).
Row 6: [K3, k4b] seven times, k1.
Rows 7 to 11: St st five rows (starting with a p row).
Row 12: K1, [k4b, k3] seven times.
Rows 13 to 60: Rep Rows 1 to 12 four times more.
Row 61: P to end.
Cast (bind) off.

The motion of the wind creates a circulation at the surface of the sea. As the water shallows, drag at the bottom of the sea causes the circulation to collapse over, forming a breaking wave. The pattern is recreated here using reverse-side stocking (stockinette) stitch to represent the white water of the breaking wave.

One-piece blanket

Repeat each row across the blanket as many times as required for the size you are making.

*Rows 1 to 3: St st three rows.
Row 4: P11, k14, p11.
Row 5: K9, p18, k9.
Row 6: P7, k22, p7.
Row 7: K6, p24, k6.
Row 8: P5, k26, p5.
Row 9: K4, p2, k24, p2, k4.
Row 10: K5, p26, k5.
Rows 11 to 15: St st five rows.
Row 16: P20, k14, p2.
Row 17: P18, k18.
Row 18: K2, p14, k20.
Row 19: P21, k12, p3.
Row 20: K4, p10, k22.
Row 21: K21, p2, k8, p2, k3.
Row 22: P4, k10, p22.
Row 23 to 27: St st five rows.
Row 28: P2, k14, p20.
Row 29: K18, p18.
Row 30: K20, p14, k2.
Row 31: P3, k12, p21.
Row 32: K22, p10, k4.

Row 33: K3, p2, k8, p2, k21.
Row 34: P22, k10, p4.
Rows 35 to 39: St st five rows.
Row 40: K7, p22, k7.
Row 41: P9, k18, p9.
Row 42: K11, p14, k11.
Row 43: P12, k12, p12.
Row 44: K13, p10, k13.
Row 45: K12, p2, k8, p2, k12.
Row 46: P13, k10, p13.
Rows 47 and 48: St st two rows**.

Individual squares

Cast on 36 sts.

Work from * to **.

Row 49: K to end.
Cast (bind) off purlwise.

48	1	2	3	4	5	6	7	8	9	10	11	12	13	14	15	16	17	18	19	20	21	22	23	24	25	26	27	28	29	30	31	32	33	34	35	36	48
47																																					47
46			13										x	x	x	x	x	10	x	x	x	x	x											13			46
45			12										x	x				8					x	x										12			45
44	x	x	13	x	x	x	x	x	x	x	x	x	x	x				10						x	x	x	x	x	x	x	x	x	x	13	x	x	44
43	x	x	12	x	x	x	x	x	x	x	x	x						12							x	x	x	x	x	x	x	x	x	12	x	x	43
42	x	x	11	x	x	x	x	x	x	x	x	x	x					14								x	x	x	x	x	x	x	x	11	x	x	42
41	x	x	9	x	x	x	x	x	x	x								18													x	x	x	9	x	x	41
40	x	x	7	x	x	x	x	x										22														x	x	7	x	x	40
39																																					39
38																																					38
37																																					37
36																																					36
35																																					35
34									22															x	x	x	x	x	x	10	x	x	x	x	x		34
33									21													x	x							8		x	x				33
32	x	x	x	x	x	x	x	x	22	x	x	x	x	x	x	x	x	x	x	x	x	x	x							10			x	x	x	x	32
31	x	x	x	x	x	x	x	x	21	x	x	x	x	x	x	x	x	x	x	x	x									12				x	x	x	31
30	x	x	x	x	x	x	x	x	20	x	x	x	x	x	x	x	x	x	x	x										14					x	x	30
29	x	x	x	x	x	x	x	x	18	x	x	x	x	x	x	x	x	x												18							29
28		x	x	x	x	x	x	x	14	x	x	x	x	x	x	x	x													20							28
27																																					27
26																																					26
25																																					25
24																																					24
23																																					23
22						x	x	x	x	10	x	x	x	x	x												22										22
21				x	x					8				x	x												21										21
20	x	x	x	x						10						x	x	x	x	x	x	x	x	x	x	x	22	x	x	x	x	x	x	x	x	x	20
19	x	x	x							12								x	x	x	x	x	x	x	x	x	21	x	x	x	x	x	x	x	x	x	19
18	x	x								14							x	x	x	x	x	x	x	x	x	x	20	x	x	x	x	x	x	x	x	x	18
17										18						x	x	x	x	x	x	x	x	x	x	x	18	x	x	x	x	x	x	x	x		17
16										20					x	x	x	x	x	x	x	x	x	x	x	x	14	x	x	x	x	x	x				16
15																																					15
14																																					14
13																																					13
12																																					12
11																																					11
10	x	x	5	x	x														26													x	x	5	x	x	10
9			4		x	x													24												x	x		4			9
8			5				x	x	x	x	x	x	x	x	x	x	x	x	26	x	x	x	x	x	x	x	x	x	x	x	x			5			8
7			6					x	x	x	x	x	x	x	x	x	x	x	24	x	x	x	x	x	x	x	x	x	x	x				6			7
6			7						x	x	x	x	x	x	x	x	x	x	22	x	x	x	x	x	x	x	x	x	x					7			6
5			9							x	x	x	x	x	x	x	x	x	18	x	x	x	x	x	x	x	x							9			5
4			11									x	x	x	x	x	x	x	14	x	x	x	x	x	x	x								11			4
3																																					3
2																																					2
1																																					1

Bottom column numbering: 36 35 34 33 32 31 30 29 28 27 26 25 24 23 22 21 20 19 18 17 16 15 14 13 12 11 10 9 8 7 6 5 4 3 2 1

One-piece blanket

Repeat each row across the blanket as many times as required for the size you are making.

*Rows 1 to 3: St st three rows.
Row 4: P15, k6, p15.
Row 5: K13, p10, k13.
Row 6: P11, k14, p11.
Row 7: K10, p16, k10.
Row 8: P9, k18, p9.
Row 9: K8, p2, k16, p2, k8.
Row 10: K9, p18, k9.
Rows 11 to 15: St st five rows.
Row 16: P24, k6, p6.
Row 17: K4, p10, k22.
Row 18: P20, k14, p2.
Row 19: K1, p16, k19.
Row 20: P18, k18.
Row 21: P1, k16, p2, k16, p1.
Row 22: K18, p18.
Row 23 to 27: St st five rows.
Row 28: P6, k6, p24.
Row 29: K22, p10, k4.
Row 30: P2, k14, p20.
Row 31: K19, p16, k1.

Row 32: K18, p18.
Row 33: P1, k16, p2, k16, p1.
Row 34: P18, k18.
Rows 35 to 39: St st five rows.
Row 40: K3, p30, k3.
Row 41: P5, k26, p5.
Row 42: K7, p22, k7.
Row 43: P8, k20, p8.
Row 44: K9, p18, k9.
Row 45: K8, p2, k16, p2, k8.
Row 46: P9, k18, p9.
Rows 47 and 48: St st two rows**.

Individual squares

Cast on 36 sts.

Work from * to **.

Row 49: K to end.

Cast (bind) off purlwise.

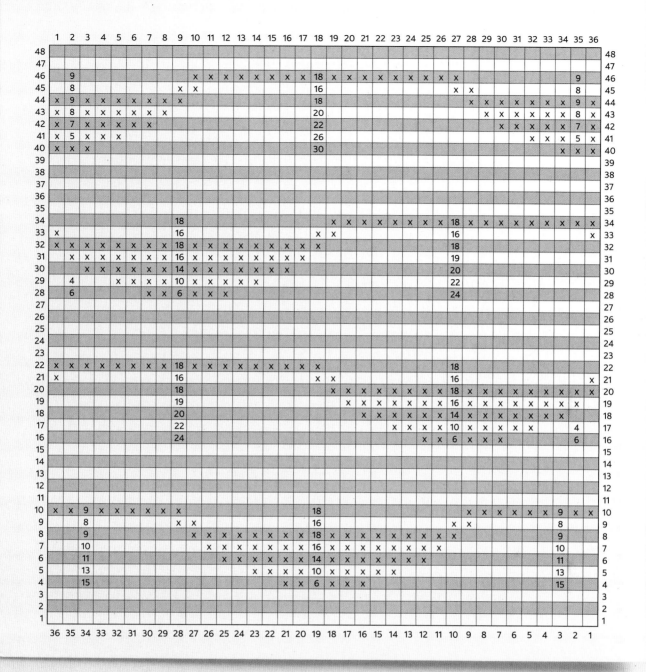

Watching waves breaking is quite hypnotic; seeing the wave grow as the water shallows and trying to guess the point at which it will break. This square represents an earlier phase of the breaking wave compared to the Large Breaking Waves square.

COMBINED BREAKING WAVES

One-piece blanket

Repeat each row across the blanket as many times as required for the size you are making.

*Rows 1 to 3: St st three rows.
Row 4: P11, k14, p11.
Row 5: K9, p18, k9.
Row 6: P7, k22, p7.
Row 7: K6, p24, k6.
Row 8: P5, k26, p5.
Row 9: K4, p2, k24, p2, k4.
Row 10: K5, p26, k5.
Rows 11 to 15: St st five rows.
Row 16: P20, k14, p2.
Row 17: P18, k18.
Row 18: K2, p14, k20.
Row 19: P21, k12, p3.
Row 20: K4, p10, k22.
Row 21: K21, p2, k8, p2, k3.
Row 22: P4, k10, p22.
Row 23 to 27: St st five rows.
Row 28: P6, k6, p24.
Row 29: K22, p10, k4.
Row 30: P2, k14, p20.
Row 31: K19, p16, k1.
Row 32: K18, p18.
Row 33: P1, k16, p2, k16, p1.
Row 34: P18, k18.
Rows 35 to 39: St st five rows.
Row 40: K3, p30, k3.
Row 41: P5, k26, p5.
Row 42: K7, p22, k7.
Row 43: P8, k20, p8.
Row 44: K9, p18, k9.

Row 45: K8, p2, k16, p2, k8.
Row 46: P9, k18, p9.
Rows 47 and 48: St st two rows**.

Individual squares

Cast on 36 sts.
Work from * to **.
Row 49: K to end.
Cast (bind) off purlwise.

	1	2	3	4	5	6	7	8	9	10	11	12	13	14	15	16	17	18	19	20	21	22	23	24	25	26	27	28	29	30	31	32	33	34	35	36	
48																																					48
47																																					47
46		9							x	x	x	x	x	x	x	x	x	18	x	x	x	x	x	x	x	x	x								9		46
45		8							x	x								16										x	x						8		45
44	x	9	x	x	x	x	x	x	x									18									x	x	x	x	x	x	x	x	9	x	44
43	x	8	x	x	x	x	x	x										20										x	x	x	x	x	x	8	x		43
42	x	7	x	x	x	x	x	x										22											x	x	x	x	x	7	x		42
41	x	5	x	x	x													26												x	x	x	5	x			41
40	x	x	x															30													x	x	x				40
39																																					39
38																																					38
37																																					37
36																																					36
35																																					35
34										18									x	x	x	x	x	x	x	x	x	18	x	x	x	x	x	x	x	x	34
33	x									16							x	x										16								x	33
32	x	x	x	x	x	x	x	x	x	18	x	x	x	x	x	x	x	x										18									32
31		x	x	x	x	x	x	x	x	16	x	x	x	x	x	x	x											19									31
30		x	x	x	x	x	x	x	x	14	x	x	x	x	x	x												20									30
29		4			x	x	x	x	x	10	x	x	x	x	x													22									29
28		6					x	x	x	6	x	x	x															24									28
27																																					27
26																																					26
25																																					25
24																																					24
23																																					23
22		4				x	x	x	x	10	x	x	x	x								22															22
21				x	x					8					x	x						21															21
20	x	4	x	x						10							x	x	x	x	x	22	x	x	x	x	x	x	x	x	x	x	x	x	x	x	20
19	x	x	x							12								x	x	x	x	21	x	x	x	x	x	x	x	x	x	x	x	x	x	x	19
18	x	x								14									x	x	x	20	x	x	x	x	x	x	x	x	x	x	x	x	x	x	18
17										18										x	x	18	x	x	x	x	x	x	x	x	x	x	x	x	x	x	17
16										20										x	x	14	x	x	x	x	x	x	x	x	x	x	x	x	x	x	16
15																																					15
14																																					14
13																																					13
12																																					12
11																																					11
10	x	x	5	x	x															26													x	x	5	x	10
9			4			x	x													24												x	x		4		9
8			5					x	x	x	x	x	x	x	x	x	x	x	x	26	x	x	x	x	x	x	x	x	x	x	x			5		8
7			6						x	x	x	x	x	x	x	x	x	x	x	24	x	x	x	x	x	x	x	x	x	x				6		7
6			7							x	x	x	x	x	x	x	x	x	x	22	x	x	x	x	x	x	x	x	x					7		6
5			9									x	x	x	x	x	x	x	x	18	x	x	x	x	x	x	x	x						9		5
4			11											x	x	x	x	x	x	14	x	x	x	x	x	x	x							11		4
3																																					3
2																																					2
1																																					1
	36	35	34	33	32	31	30	29	28	27	26	25	24	23	22	21	20	19	18	17	16	15	14	13	12	11	10	9	8	7	6	5	4	3	2	1	

One-piece blanket

Repeat each row across the blanket as many times as required for the size you are making. Note: if you have a hard colour change against the previous square, knit across Row 1 for a neater join, instead of working the pattern row.

*Row 1: K2, p1, k2, p8, [k3, p1] twice, k2, p8, k3, p1, k1.

Row 2: P1, k1, p3, k8, p2, [k1, p3] twice, k8, p2, k1, p2.

Row 3: K2, p1, k2, p8, [k3, p1] twice, k2, p8, k3, p1, k1.

Row 4: K1, p1, k3, p1, k9, [p1, k3] twice, p1, k9, p1, k2.

Row 5: P1, k3, p8, k2, [p1, k3] twice, p8, k2, p1, k3.

Row 6: P3, k1, p2, k8, [p3, k1] twice, p2, k8, p3, k1.

Row 7: P1, k3, p8, k2, [p1, k3] twice, p8, k2, p1, k3.

Row 8: K3, p1, k9, [p1, k3] twice, p1, k9, p1, k3, p1.

Rows 9 to 48: Rep Rows 1 to 8 five times more**.

Individual squares

Cast on 36 sts.

Work from * to **.

Cast (bind) off.

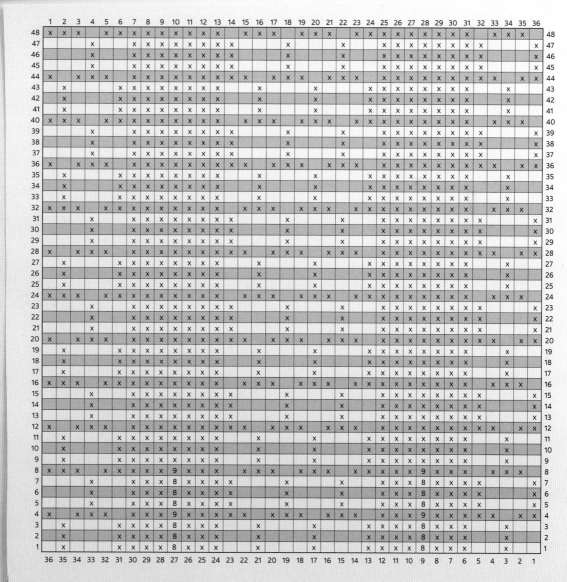

PALM TREE FRONDS

The sight of palm tree fronds waving in the breeze always suggests the tropics, even if the sky above is not so sunny! This is quite a complex pattern with lots of stitch changes to represent the feathery fronds, so you will need to pay attention as you work it.

One-piece blanket

Repeat each row across the blanket as many times as required for the size you are making. Note: if you have a hard colour change against the previous square, knit across Row 1 for a neater join, instead of working the pattern row.

*Row 1: P4, k9, p9, k9, p5.
Row 2: K4, p11, k7, p11, k3.
Row 3: P4, [k1, p1] four times, k1, p9, [k1, p1] four times, k1, p5.
Row 4: K4, [p1, k1] five times, p1, k7, [p1, k1] five times, p1, k3.
Row 5: P2, k1, p29, k1, p3.
Row 6: K4, [p1, k1] five times, p1, k7, [p1, k1] five times, p1, k3.
Row 7: P2, [k1, p1] six times, k1, p5, [k1, p1] six times, k1, p3.
Row 8: K2, p9, [k1, p1] three times, k3, [p1, k1] three times, p9, k1.
Row 9: K9, [p1, k1] twice, p2, k1, p3, k1, p2, [k1, p1] twice, k10.
Row 10: P9, [k1, p1] twice, [k3, p1] three times, k1, p1, k1, p8.
Row 11: K7, [p1, k1] four times, p5, [k1, p1] four times, k8.
Row 12: P7, [k1, p1] twice, k4, p1, k5, p1, k4, [p1, k1] twice, p6.
Row 13: K5, [p1, k1] twice, [p2, k1, p1, k1] four times, p1, k6.
Row 14: P5, [k1, p1] three times, k3, p2, k5, p2, k3, [p1, k1] three times, p4.
Row 15: K3, [p1, k1] 14 times, p1, k4.

Row 16: P3, [k1, p1] twice, k1, p2, [k3, p1, k2, p1] twice, k3, p2, [k1, p1] twice, k1, p2.
Row 17: [K1, p1] three times, k2, [p1, k1] three times, [p2, k1, p1, k1] twice, p1, k1, p1, k2, [p1, k1] twice, p1, k2.
Row 18: P3, k1, p1, k1, p3, k3, p2, k2, p1, k3, p1, k2, p2, k3, p3, k1, p1, k1, p2.
Row 19: [K1, p1] twice, k3, [p1, k1] twice, [p2, k1] twice, p1, k1, [p2, k1] twice, p1, k1, p1, k3, p1, k1, p1, k2.
Row 20: P8, k3, p2, [k3, p1] twice, k3, p2, k3, p7.
Row 21: K6, [p1, k1] twice, p2, [k1, p1] five times, k1, p2, [k1, p1] twice, k7.
Row 22: P7, k3, p3, [k3, p1] twice, k3, p3, k3, p6.
Row 23: K5, [p1, k1] 12 times, p1, k6.
Row 24: P6, k3, p3, [k3, p2] twice, k3, p3, k3, p5.
Row 25: K4, [p1, k1] five times, p2, k1, p1, k1, p2, [k1, p1] five times, k5.
Row 26: P5, k3, p4, [k3, p2] twice, [k3, p4] twice.
Row 27: K3, [p1, k1] twice, p1, k2, [p1, k1] twice, [p2, k1, p1, k1] twice, p1, k2, [p1, k1] twice, p1, k4.
Row 28: [P4, k3] twice, [p3, k3] twice, p4, k3, p3.

Row 29: K2, [p1, k1] twice, p1, k2, [p1, k1] eight times, p1, k2, [p1, k1] twice, p1, k3.
Row 30: P3, k3, p5, [k3, p3] twice, k3, p5, k3, p2.
Row 31: [K1, p1] three times, k3, [p1, k1] eight times, p1, k3, [p1, k1] twice, p1, k2.
Row 32: P3, k3, [p4, k3] four times, p2.
Row 33: K8, [p1, k1] twice, p1, k2, [p1, k1] twice, p1, k2, [p1, k1] twice, p1, k9.
Row 34: P10, [k3, p4] twice, k3, p9.
Row 35: K8, [p1, k1] twice, p1, k2, [p1, k1] twice, p1, k2, [p1, k1] twice, p1, k9.
Row 36: P9, [k3, p5] twice, k3, p8.
Row 37: K7, [p1, k1] twice, p1, k3, [p1, k1] twice, p1, k3, [p1, k1] twice, p1, k8.
Row 38: P9, [k3, p5] twice, k3, p8.

Row 39: K7, [p1, k1] twice, p1, k3, [p1, k1] twice, p1, k3, [p1, k1] twice, p1, k8.
Row 40: P9, k1, p1, k1, p5, k3, p5, k1, p1, k1, p8.
Row 41: K15, [p1, k1] twice, p1, k16.
Row 42: P17, k3, p16.
Row 43: K15, [p1, k1] twice, p1, k16.
Row 44: P17, k3, p16.
Row 45: K15, [p1, k1] twice, p1, k16.
Row 46: P17, k1, p1, k1, p16.
Rows 47 and 48: St st two rows**.

Individual squares

Cast on 36 sts.

Work from * to **.

Cast (bind) off.

Forest

Forests contain a wide variety of textures in tree trunk bark and in leaf shapes. I have specified bark types for different tree types, but there is a lot of cross-over between species, so you can choose your favourite. Leaf patterns in this section aim to reproduce the shape of leaves in a representative way, rather than a direct reproduction of trees in a forest. The leaves at the base of the tree start large then decrease in size up the blanket as they appear to get further away. Stalks in leaf patterns repeat vertically between squares, so if you are joining different sizes you will need the alternative rows in the instructions. In a deciduous forest, the different greens often get lighter as you go up the tree canopy. Alternatively you could use reds, oranges and browns to create an autumnal scene.

The first four patterns are based on a beech tree, but could represent any oval shaped leaf, such as alder or elm. **Beech Tree Trunks** has smooth bark with occasional horizontal markings. **Medium Beech Leaves** incorporates the fruit, which is a small nut called a 'mast' inside a rough shell or 'burr'. The burrs fall from the tree in autumn, slowly opening over time.

The next four patterns represent maple trees, a broad family covering a variety of species. Maples are known for their stunning range of autumn colours, especially in eastern North America. The patterns here are based on the sycamore, a tree in the maple family native to Central Europe, but found throughout Europe, North America and Australasia. The bark of a sycamore is smooth when the tree is young, but becomes more gnarly as the tree ages – see **Maple Tree Trunks**. **Medium Maple Leaves** includes the distinctive winged seeds called 'samaras', which rotate as they fall, gaining the nickname 'helicopter' seeds, to help them fly further to disperse the seeds.

The next patterns represent oak trees, which have a variety of bark and lobed leaf shapes. They are culturally significant in many countries, used as a symbol of strength and endurance. **Oak Tree Trunks** has distinctive curvy, forked vertical ridges, but in some species they are more similar to the sycamore. An acorn is represented on **Medium Oak Leaves**. The acorns are dispersed by squirrels and other animals as they cache them in the soil for winter.

The final three patterns are a mixture of all three leaf patterns, which could be combined with a mix of trunk patterns to produce a broadleaved forest.

One-piece blanket

Repeat each row across the blanket as many times as required for the size you are making. Note: if you have a hard colour change against the previous square, knit across Row 1 for a neater join, instead of working the pattern row.

*Row 1: P3, k11, p7, k11, p4.
Row 2: K4, p11, k7, p11, k3.
Rows 3 and 4: Rep Rows 1 and 2.
Row 5: P3, k1, p5, k5, p7, k1, p5, k5, p4.
Row 6: K4, p11, k7, p11, k3.
Row 7: P3, k11, p7, k11, p4.
Rows 8 to 11: Rep Rows 6 and 7 twice more.
Row 12: K4, p11, k7, p11, k3.

Row 13: P3, k5, p5, k1, p7, k5, p5, k1, p4.
Row 14: K4, p11, k7, p11, k3.
Row 15: P3, k11, p7, k11, p4.
Row 16 to 19: Rep Rows 14 and 15 twice more.
Row 20: K4, p11, k7, p11, k3.
Row 21: P3, k3, p5, k3, p7, k3, p5, k3, p4.
Rows 22 and 23: Rep Rows 14 and 15.
Row 24: K4, p11, k7, p11, k3.
Rows 25 to 48: Rep Rows 1 to 24**.

Individual squares

Cast on 36 sts.

Work from * to **.

Cast (bind) off.

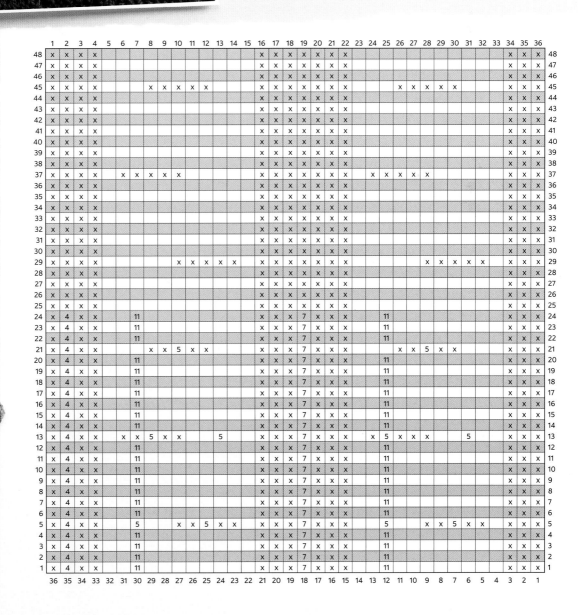

Beech leaves are simple oval-shaped leaves with a smooth surface, meaning that they are best represented with the smoother right-side stocking (stockinette) stitch. As a result, the leaves need to be oriented vertically for the leaf texture to show in relief on the right-side.

One-piece blanket

Repeat each row across the blanket as many times as required for the size you are making. Note: if you have a hard colour change against the previous square, knit across Row 1 for a neater join, instead of working the pattern row.

To join to large or medium leaf patterns:

*__Row 1__: [P8, k1] four times.
__Row 2__: [P1, k8] four times.
__Row 3__: [P8, k1] four times.
__Row 4__: K7, p5, k13, p5, k6.
__Row 5__: P5, k7, p11, k7, p6.
__Row 6__: K5, p9, k9, p9, k4.
__Row 7__: P3, k11, p7, k11, p4.
__Row 8__: K4, p11, k7, p11, k3.
__Row 9__: P2, k13, p5, k13, p3.
__Row 10__: K3, p13, k5, p13, k2.
Rows 11 to 16: Rep Rows 9 and 10 three times more.
__Row 17__: P2, k13, p5, k13, p3.
__Row 18__: K4, p11, k7, p11, k3.
__Row 19__: P3, k11, p7, k11, p4.
__Row 20__: K5, p9, k9, p9, k4.
__Row 21__: P4, k9, p9, k9, p5.
__Row 22__: K6, p7, k11, p7, k5.
__Row 23__: P6, k5, p13, k5, p7.
__Row 24__: [P1, k7, p3, k7] twice.
__Row 25__: [K1, p7] twice, k3, p7, k1, p7, k2.
__Row 26__: P3, k13, p5, k13, p2.
__Row 27__: K3, p11, k7, p11, k4.
__Row 28__: P5, k9, p9, k9, p4.
__Row 29__: K4, p9, k9, p9, k5.
__Row 30__: P6, k7, p11, k7, p5.
__Row 31__: K5, p7, k11, p7, k6.
__Row 32__: P7, k5, p13, k5, p6.
__Row 33__: K6, p5, k13, p5, k7.
Rows 34 to 39: Rep Rows 32 and 33 three times more.
__Row 40__: P7, k5, p13, k5, p6.
__Row 41__: K5, p7, k11, p7, k6.
__Row 42__: P6, k7, p11, k7, p5.
__Row 43__: K4, p9, k9, p9, k5.
__Row 44__: P4, k11, p7, k11, p3.
__Row 45__: K2, p13, k5, p13, k3.
__Row 46__: [P1, k8] four times.
__Row 47__: [P8, k1] four times.
__Row 48__: [P1, k8] four times**.*

To join below small leaf patterns:

Rows 1 to 45: Work as Rows 1 to 45 above.
__Row 46__: [P1, k17] twice.
__Row 47__: P5, k1, p23, k1, p5, k1.
__Row 48__: P1, k5, [p1, k11] twice, p1, k5.

Individual squares

Cast on 36 sts.

Work from * to **.

Cast (bind) off.

To join below small leaf patterns:

	1	2	3	4	5	6	7	8	9	10	11	12	13	14	15	16	17	18	19	20	21	22	23	24	25	26	27	28	29	30	31	32	33	34	35	36	
48		x	x	5	x	x		x	x	x	x	x	x	11	x	x	x	x	x		x	x	x	x	11	x	x	x	x	x		x	x	5	x	x	48
47		x	x	5	x	x		x	x	x	x	x	x	x	x	x	x	x	x		x	x	x	23	x	x	x	x	x			x	x	5	x	x	47
46		x	x	x	x	x	x	x	x	x	x	x	17	x	x	x	x	x		x	x	x	x	17	x	x	x	x	x	x		x	x	x	x		46

To join to large or medium leaf patterns:

	1	2	3	4	5	6	7	8	9	10	11	12	13	14	15	16	17	18	19	20	21	22	23	24	25	26	27	28	29	30	31	32	33	34	35	36	
48		x	x	x	8	x	x	x	x	x		x	x	x	8	x	x	x		x	x	x	8	x	x	x	x		x	x	x	8	x	x	x	x	48
47		x	x	x	8	x	x	x	x			x	x	x	8	x	x	x		x	x	x	8	x	x	x			x	x	x	8	x	x	x		47
46		x	x	x	8	x	x	x	x			x	x	x	8	x	x	x		x	x	x	8	x	x	x			x	x	x	8	x	x	x	x	46
45			x	x	x	x	x	x	x	13	x	x	x	x	x	x		5			x	x	x	x	x	x	13	x	x	x	x	x	x				45
44		4			x	x	x	x	x	11	x	x	x	x	x			7				x	x	x	x	x	11	x	x	x	x	x					44
43		5				x	x	x	x	9	x	x	x	x				9					x	x	x	x	9	x	x	x	x				4		43
42		6					x	x	x	7	x	x	x					11					x	x	x	7	x	x	x						5		42
41		6					x	x	x	7	x	x	x					11					x	x	x	7	x	x	x						5		41
40		7						x	x	5	x	x						13						x	x	5	x	x							6		40
39		7						x	x	5	x	x						13						x	x	5	x	x							6		39
38		7						x	x	5	x	x						13						x	x	5	x	x							6		38
37		7						x	x	5	x	x						13						x	x	5	x	x							6		37
36		7						x	x	5	x	x						13						x	x	5	x	x							6		36
35		7						x	x	5	x	x						13						x	x	5	x	x							6		35
34		7						x	x	5	x	x						13						x	x	5	x	x							6		34
33		7						x	x	5	x	x						13						x	x	5	x	x							6		33
32		7						x	x	5	x	x						13						x	x	5	x	x							6		32
31		6					x	x	x	7	x	x	x					11					x	x	x	7	x	x	x						5		31
30		6					x	x	x	7	x	x	x					11					x	x	x	7	x	x	x						5		30
29		5				x	x	x	x	9	x	x	x	x				9					x	x	x	x	9	x	x	x	x				4		29
28		5				x	x	x	x	9	x	x	x	x				9					x	x	x	x	9	x	x	x	x				4		28
27		4			x	x	x	x	x	11	x	x	x	x	x			7				x	x	x	x	x	11	x	x	x	x	x					27
26			x	x	x	x	x	x	x	13	x	x	x	x	x	x		5			x	x	x	x	x	x	13	x	x	x	x	x	x				26
25				x	x	x	7	x	x	x			x	x	x	7	x	x	x			x	x	x	7	x	x	x		x	x	x	7	x	x	x	25
24		x	x	x	7	x	x	x				x	x	x	7	x	x	x		x	x	x	7	x	x	x			x	x	x	7	x	x	x		24
23	x	x	7	x	x	x	x			5			x	x	x	x	x	x	13	x	x	x	x	x		5			x	x	x	x	6	x	x		23
22	x	x	6	x	x	x				7				x	x	x	x	x	11	x	x	x	x			7				x	x	x	5	x	x		22
21	x	x	5	x	x					9					x	x	x	x	9	x	x	x	x			9					x	4	x	x		21
20	x	x	5	x	x					9					x	x	x	x	9	x	x	x	x			9					x	4	x	x		20
19	x	x	4	x						11						x	x	x	7	x	x	x				11						x	x	x		19
18	x	x	4	x						11						x	x	x	7	x	x	x				11						x	x	x		18
17	x	x	x							13							x	x	5	x	x					13							x	x		17
16	x	x	x							13							x	x	5	x	x					13							x	x		16
15	x	x	x							13							x	x	5	x	x					13							x	x		15
14	x	x	x							13							x	x	5	x	x					13							x	x		14
13	x	x	x							13							x	x	5	x	x					13							x	x		13
12	x	x	x							13							x	x	5	x	x					13							x	x		12
11	x	x	x							13							x	x	5	x	x					13							x	x		11
10	x	x	x							13							x	x	5	x	x					13							x	x		10
9	x	x	x							13							x	x	5	x	x					13							x	x		9
8	x	x	4	x						11						x	x	x	7	x	x	x				11						x	x	x		8
7	x	x	4	x						11						x	x	x	7	x	x	x				11						x	x	x		7
6	x	x	5	x	x					9					x	x	x	x	9	x	x	x	x			9					x	4	x	x		6
5	x	x	x	x	6	x				7			x	x	x	x	x	11	x	x	x	x	x			7			x	x	x	5	x	x		5
4	x	x	x	x	7	x	x			5			x	x	x	x	x	13	x	x	x	x	x	x		5			x	x	x	6	x	x		4
3		x	x	x	8	x	x	x	x		x	x	x	x	8	x	x	x		x	x	x	8	x	x	x		x	x	x	8	x	x	x	x		3
2		x	x	x	8	x	x	x	x		x	x	x	x	8	x	x	x		x	x	x	8	x	x	x		x	x	x	8	x	x	x	x		2
1		x	x	x	8	x	x	x	x		x	x	x	x	8	x	x	x		x	x	x	8	x	x	x		x	x	x	8	x	x	x	x		1

36	35	34	33	32	31	30	29	28	27	26	25	24	23	22	21	20	19	18	17	16	15	14	13	12	11	10	9	8	7	6	5	4	3	2	1

As a child, my walk home would take me past a beech tree; I would pick up a burr and put it in the pocket of my big winter coat waiting for it to open. I wanted to incorporate the burrs in this square design, so they fill the space in between the medium size beech leaves.

One-piece blanket

Repeat each row across the blanket as many times as required for the size you are making. Note: if you have a hard colour change against the previous square, knit across Row 1 for a neater join, instead of working the pattern row.

To join to large or medium leaf patterns:

*Row 1: [P8, k1] four times.
Row 2: [P1, k8] four times.
Row 3: [P8, k1] four times.
Row 4: K7, p5, k13, p5, k6.
Row 5: P5, k7, p11, k7, p6.
Row 6: K5, p9, k9, p9, k4.
Row 7: P4, k9, p9, k9, p5.
Row 8: K4, p11, k7, p11, k3.
Row 9: P3, k11, p7, k11, p4.
Rows 10 to 13: Rep Rows 8 and 9 twice more.
Row 14: K4, p11, k7, p11, k3.
Row 15: P4, k9, p9, k9, p5.
Row 16: K5, p9, k9, p9, k4.
Row 17: P5, k7, p11, k7, p6.
Row 18: K6, p7, k11, p7, k5.
Row 19: P3, k1, p2, k5, p2, k1, p7, k1, p2, k5, p2, k1, p4.
Row 20: K3, [p3, k2] twice, p3, k5, [p3, k2] three times.
Row 21: [P1, k1] three times, [p2, k1] twice, [p1, k1] twice, p3, [k1, p1] twice, [k1, p2] twice, [k1, p1] twice, k1, p2.
Row 22: K2, p5, k5, p5, k3, p5, k5, p5, k1.
Row 23: P1, k5, p5, k5, p3, k5, p5, k5, p2.

Row 24: K2, p5, k5, p5, k3, p5, k5, p5, k1.
Row 25: P2, k3, p7, k3, p5, k3, p7, k3, p3.
Row 26: K3, p3, k7, p3, k5, p3, k7, p3, k2.
Row 27: P3, [k1, p4] twice, k1, p7, [k1, p4] three times.
Row 28: [P1, k3] twice, p3, k3, [p1, k3] three times, p3, k3, p1, k3.
Row 29: [K1, p2] twice, [k1, p1] twice, [k1, p2] twice, k3, [p2, k1] twice, [p1, k1] twice, p2, k1, p2, k2.
Row 30: P3, [k4, p5] three times, k4, p2.
Row 31: K3, p3, k5, p3, k7, p3, k5, p3, k4.
Row 32: P4, k3, p5, k3, p7, k3, p5, k3, p3.
Row 33: K4, p3, k3, p3, k9, p3, k3, p3, k5.
Row 34: P5, k3, p3, k3, p9, k3, p3, k3, p4.
Row 35: K5, p3, k1, p3, k11, p3, k1, p3, k6.
Row 36: P6, k3, p1, k3, p11, k3, p1, k3, p5.
Row 37: K5, p3, k1, p3, k11, p3, k1, p3, k6.
Row 38: P6, k7, p11, k7, p5.
Row 39: K5, p7, k11, p7, k6.
Row 40 and 41: Rep Rows 38 and 39.
Row 42: P5, k9, p9, k9, p4.
Row 43: K4, p9, k9, p9, k5.
Row 44: P4, k11, p7, k11, p3.

Row 45: K2, p13, k5, p13, k3.
Row 46: [P1, k8] four times.
Row 47: [P8, k1] four times.
Row 48: [P1, k8] four times**.

To join below small leaf patterns:

Rows 1–45: Work as Rows 1–45 above.
Row 46: [P1, k17] twice.
Row 47: P5, k1, p23, k1, p5, k1.
Row 48: P1, k5, [p1, k11] twice, p1, k5.

Individual squares

Cast on 36 sts.
Work from * to **.
Cast (bind) off.

To join below small leaf patterns:

	1	2	3	4	5	6	7	8	9	10	11	12	13	14	15	16	17	18	19	20	21	22	23	24	25	26	27	28	29	30	31	32	33	34	35	36	
48		x	x	5	x	x		x	x	x	x	x	x	11	x	x	x	x	x	x		x	x	x	x	x	11	x	x	x	x	x	x		x	x	5	x	x	48
47		x	x	5	x	x		x	x	x	x	x	x	x	x	x	x	x	x	x	23	x	x	x	x	x	x		x	x	5	x	x	47
46		x	x	x	x	x	x		x	x	x	x	17	x	x	x	x	x		x	x	x	x	x	x	17	x	x	x	x	x	x	x	x	46

To join to large or medium leaf patterns:

	1	2	3	4	5	6	7	8	9	10	11	12	13	14	15	16	17	18	19	20	21	22	23	24	25	26	27	28	29	30	31	32	33	34	35	36	
48		x	8	x	x	x	x	x	x	x	x	x	x	x	x	x	8	x	x	8	x	x	x	x	x	x	x	x	x	x	x	x	8	x	48
47		x	8	x	x	x	x	x	x	x	x	x	x	x	x	x	8	x	x	8	x	x	x	x	x	x	x	x	x	x	x	x	8	x	47
46		x	8	x	x	x	x	x	x	x	x	x	x	x	x	x	8	x	x	8	x	x	x	x	x	x	x	x	x	x	x	x	8	x	46
45	45
44	44
43	43
42	42
41	41
40	40
39	39
38	38
37	37
36	36
35	35
34	34
33	33
32	32
31	31
30	30
29	29
28	28
27	27
26	26
25	25
24	24
23	23
22	22
21	21
20	20
19	19
18	18
17	17
16	16
15	15
14	14
13	13
12	12
11	11
10	10
9	9
8	8
7	7
6	6
5	5
4	4
3	3
2	2
1	1

Bottom column numbering (right to left): 36 35 34 33 32 31 30 29 28 27 26 25 24 23 22 21 20 19 18 17 16 15 14 13 12 11 10 9 8 7 6 5 4 3 2 1

SMALL BEECH LEAVES

One-piece blanket

Repeat each row across the blanket as many times as required for the size you are making. Note: if you have a hard colour change against the previous square, knit across Row 1 for a neater join, instead of working the pattern row.

To join to small leaf patterns:
*****Row 1**: [P5, k1] six times.
Row 2: [P1, k4, p3, k4] three times.
Row 3: [P3, k5, p3, k1] three times.
Row 4: K4, [p5, k7] twice, p5, k3.
Row 5: P2, [k7, p5] twice, k7, p3.
Row 6: K3, [p7, k5] twice, p7, k2.
Row 7 and 8: Rep Rows 5 and 6.
Row 9: P2, [k7, p5] twice, k7, p3.
Row 10: K4, [p5, k7] twice, p5, k3.
Row 11: P3, [k5, p7] twice, k5, p4.
Row 12: [P1, k4, p3, k4] three times.
Row 13: K1, [p3, k3] five times, p3, k2.
Row 14: P2, [k4, p1, k4, p3] twice, [k4, p1] twice.
Row 15: K2, [p7, k5] twice, p7, k3.
Row 16: P3, [k7, p5] twice, k7, p2.
Row 17: K3, [p5, k7] twice, p5, k4.

Row 18: P4, [k5, p7] twice, k5, p3.
Rows 19 and 20: Rep Rows 17 and 18.
Row 21: K3, [p5, k7] twice, p5, k4.
Row 22: P3, [k7, p5] twice, k7, p2.
Row 23: K2, [p3, k1, p3, k5] twice, p3, k1, p3, k3.
Row 24: P2, [k4, p1, k4, p3] twice, k4, p1, k4, p1.
Rows 25 to 48: Rep Rows 1 to 24**.

To join above large or medium leaf patterns:
Row 1: P5, [k1, p11] twice, k1, p5, k1.
Row 2: P1, k4, [p3, k9] twice, p3, k4.
Row 3: P3, [k5, p7] twice, k5, p3, k1.
Rows 4 to 48: Work as Rows 4 to 48 above (working Rows 1 to 3 as above for Rows 25 to 27).

Individual squares

Cast on 36 sts.

Work from * to **.

Cast (bind) off.

Small Beech Leaves follows the design of Large Beech Leaves, only smaller in size due to perspective from the ground. If you want to join these above Medium or Large Beech Leaves, you will need the alternative instructions here and for the large or medium leaf you wish to join it to.

Column headers (top): 1 2 3 4 5 6 7 8 9 10 11 12 13 14 15 16 17 18 19 20 21 22 23 24 25 26 27 28 29 30 31 32 33 34 35 36

Rows (numbered 48 down to 1 on both sides) forming a chart of x marks and occasional numbers (4, 5, 7).

Column footers (bottom): 36 35 34 33 32 31 30 29 28 27 26 25 24 23 22 21 20 19 18 17 16 15 14 13 12 11 10 9 8 7 6 5 4 3 2 1

To join above large or medium leaf patterns:

Row																																			
3	x	x	x			5			x	x	x	x	x	7	x	x	x			5			x	x	x	7	x	x	x			5			x	x	x
2	x	4	x	x				x	x	x	x	x	9	x	x	x	x			x	x	x	x	x	9	x	x	x	x			x	x	4	x	x
1	x	x	5	x	x			x	x	x	x	x	11	x	x	x	x	x		x	x	x	x	x	11	x	x	x	x	x		x	x	5	x	x

Column footers: 36 35 34 33 32 31 30 29 28 27 26 25 24 23 22 21 20 19 18 17 16 15 14 13 12 11 10 9 8 7 6 5 4 3 2 1

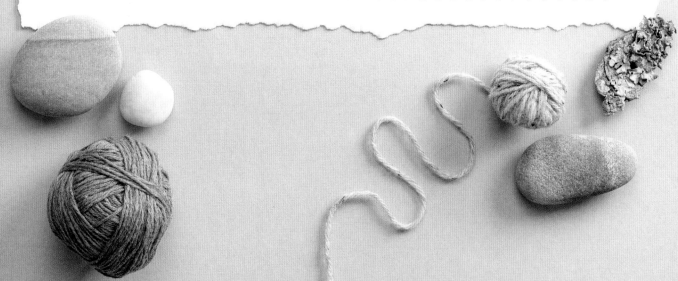

22 / MAPLE TREE TRUNKS

Some varieties of maple, such as the sugar maple, produce sap that is used to make maple syrup. The trunks are drilled and a 'tap' inserted to harvest the sap into buckets for turning into the syrup. The bark texture in this square aims to reproduce the rough bark of a mature maple tree.

One-piece blanket

Repeat each row across the blanket as many times as required for the size you are making. Note: if you have a hard colour change against the previous square, knit across Row 1 for a neater join, instead of working the pattern row.

*Row 1: P3, k11, p7, k11, p4.
Row 2: K4, p11, k7, p11, k3.
Row 3: P3, [k1, p1] five times, k1, p7, [k1, p1] five times, k1, p4.
Row 4: K4, [p1, k1] five times, p1, k7, [p1, k1] five times, p1, k3.
Rows 5 and 6: Rep Rows 1 and 2.
Row 7: P3, k2, [p1, k1] three times, p1, k2, p7, k2, [p1, k1] three times, p1, k2, p4.
Row 8: K4, p2, [k1, p1] three times, k1, p2, k7, p2, [k1, p1] three times, k1, p2, k3.
Rows 9 to 48: Rep Rows 1 to 8 five times more**.

Individual squares

Cast on 36 sts.
Work from * to **.
Cast (bind) off.

Knitting colorwork chart — 36 stitches wide × 48 rows.

	1	2	3	4	5	6	7	8	9	10	11	12	13	14	15	16	17	18	19	20	21	22	23	24	25	26	27	28	29	30	31	32	33	34	35	36	
48	x	x	x	x			x		x		x		x			x	x	x	x	x	x	x			x		x		x		x			x	x	x	48
47	x	x	x	x				x		x		x				x	x	x	x	x	x	x	x		x		x		x		x			x	x	x	47
46	x	x	x	x												x	x	x	x	x	x	x	x											x	x	x	46
45	x	x	x	x												x	x	x	x	x	x	x												x	x	x	45
44	x	x	x	x			x		x		x		x			x	x	x	x	x	x	x		x		x		x		x		x		x	x	x	44
43	x	x	x	x		x		x		x		x		x		x	x	x	x	x	x	x		x		x		x		x		x		x	x	x	43
42	x	x	x	x												x	x	x	x	x	x	x												x	x	x	42
41	x	x	x	x												x	x	x	x	x	x	x												x	x	x	41
40	x	x	x	x			x		x		x		x			x	x	x	x	x	x	x		x		x		x		x				x	x	x	40
39	x	x	x	x		x		x		x		x		x		x	x	x	x	x	x	x		x		x		x		x				x	x	x	39
38	x	x	x	x												x	x	x	x	x	x	x												x	x	x	38
37	x	x	x	x												x	x	x	x	x	x	x												x	x	x	37
36	x	x	x	x			x		x		x		x			x	x	x	x	x	x	x		x		x		x		x		x		x	x	x	36
35	x	x	x	x		x		x		x		x		x		x	x	x	x	x	x	x		x		x		x		x		x		x	x	x	35
34	x	x	x	x												x	x	x	x	x	x	x												x	x	x	34
33	x	x	x	x												x	x	x	x	x	x	x												x	x	x	33
32	x	x	x	x			x		x		x		x			x	x	x	x	x	x	x		x		x		x		x				x	x	x	32
31	x	x	x	x		x		x		x		x		x		x	x	x	x	x	x	x		x		x		x		x				x	x	x	31
30	x	x	x	x												x	x	x	x	x	x	x												x	x	x	30
29	x	x	x	x												x	x	x	x	x	x	x												x	x	x	29
28	x	x	x	x			x		x		x		x			x	x	x	x	x	x	x		x		x		x		x		x		x	x	x	28
27	x	x	x	x		x		x		x		x		x		x	x	x	x	x	x	x		x		x		x		x		x		x	x	x	27
26	x	x	x	x												x	x	x	x	x	x	x												x	x	x	26
25	x	x	x	x												x	x	x	x	x	x	x												x	x	x	25
24	x	x	x	x			x		x		x		x			x	x	x	x	x	x	x		x		x		x		x				x	x	x	24
23	x	x	x	x		x		x		x		x		x		x	x	x	x	x	x	x		x		x		x		x				x	x	x	23
22	x	x	x	x												x	x	x	x	x	x	x												x	x	x	22
21	x	x	x	x												x	x	x	x	x	x	x												x	x	x	21
20	x	x	x	x			x		x		x		x			x	x	x	x	x	x	x		x		x		x		x				x	x	x	20
19	x	x	x	x		x		x		x		x		x		x	x	x	x	x	x	x		x		x		x		x				x	x	x	19
18	x	x	x	x												x	x	x	x	x	x	x												x	x	x	18
17	x	x	x	x												x	x	x	x	x	x	x												x	x	x	17
16	x	x	x	x			x		x		x		x			x	x	x	x	x	x	x		x		x		x		x		x		x	x	x	16
15	x	x	x	x		x		x		x		x		x		x	x	x	x	x	x	x		x		x		x		x		x		x	x	x	15
14	x	x	x	x												x	x	x	x	x	x	x												x	x	x	14
13	x	x	x	x												x	x	x	x	x	x	x												x	x	x	13
12	x	x	x	x			x		x		x		x			x	x	x	x	x	x	x		x		x		x		x		x		x	x	x	12
11	x	x	x	x		x		x		x		x		x		x	x	x	x	x	x	x		x		x		x		x		x		x	x	x	11
10	x	x	x	x												x	x	x	x	x	x	x												x	x	x	10
9	x	x	x	x												x	x	x	x	x	x	x												x	x	x	9
8	x	4	x	x			x		x		x		x			x	x	x	7	x	x	x		x		x		x		x		x		x	x	x	8
7	x	4	x	x				x		x		x		x		x	x	x	7	x	x	x		x		x		x		x		x		x	x	x	7
6	x	4	x	x						11						x	x	x	7	x	x	x						11						x	x	x	6
5	x	4	x	x						11						x	x	x	7	x	x	x						11						x	x	x	5
4	x	4	x	x			x		x		x		x			x	x	x	7	x	x	x		x		x		x		x		x		x	x	x	4
3	x	4	x	x		x		x		x		x		x		x	x	x	7	x	x	x		x		x		x		x		x		x	x	x	3
2	x	4	x	x						11						x	x	x	7	x	x	x						11						x	x	x	2
1	x	4	x	x						11						x	x	x	7	x	x	x						11						x	x	x	1
	36	35	34	33	32	31	30	29	28	27	26	25	24	23	22	21	20	19	18	17	16	15	14	13	12	11	10	9	8	7	6	5	4	3	2	1	

Maple leaves are five-pointed leaves, with varying shapes and sizes. As with the beech leaf patterns, they need to be oriented vertically for the smooth leaf texture to show in relief on the right-side of the square.

One-piece blanket

Repeat each row across the blanket as many times as required for the size you are making. Note: if you have a hard colour change against the previous square, knit across Row 1 for a neater join, instead of working the pattern row.

To join to large or medium leaf patterns:

**Row 1: [P8, k1] four times.

Row 2: [P1, k8] four times.

Row 3: [P8, k1] four times.

Row 4: K5, p2, k2, p1, k2, p2, k9, p2, k2, p1, k2, p2, k4.

Row 5: P2, k5, p1, k1, p1, k5, p5, k5, p1, k1, p1, k5, p3.

Row 6: K2, p15, k3, p15, k1.

Row 7: P1, k15, p3, k15, p2.

Row 8: K3, p13, k5, p13, k2.

Row 9: P3, k11, p7, k11, p4.

Row 10: K3, p13, k5, p13, k2.

Row 11: P1, k15, p3, k15, p2.

Row 12: K2, p15, k3, p15, k1.

Rows 13 and 14: Rep Rows 11 and 12.

Row 15: P1, k15, p3, k15, p2.

Row 16: K2, p3, k1, p7, k1, p3, k3, p3, k1, p7, k1, p3, k1.

Row 17: P1, k2, p2, k7, p2, k2, p3, k2, p2, k7, p2, k2, p2.

Row 18: K2, p1, k3, p7, [k3, p1] twice, k3, p7, k3, p1, k1.

Row 19: P5, k7, p11, k7, p6.

Row 20: K7, p5, k13, p5, k6.

Row 21: P6, k5, k13, k5, p7.

Row 22: K7, p5, k13, p5, k6.

Row 23: P7, k3, p15, k3, p8.

Row 24: [P1, k7, p3, k7] twice.

Row 25: [K1, p7] twice, k3, p7, k1, p7, k2.

Row 26: P2, k15, p3, k15, p1.

Row 27: K2, p13, k5, p13, k3.

Row 28: P3, k13, p5, k13, p2.

Row 29: K2, p13, k5, p13, k3.

Row 30: P4, k11, p7, k11, p3.

Row 31: K3, [p3, k1] twice, p3, k7, [p3, k1] twice, p3, k4.

Row 32: P4, k2, p2, k3, p2, k2, p7, k2, p2, k3, p2, k2, p3.

Row 33: K3, p1, k3, p3, k3, p1, k7, p1, k3, p3, k3, p1, k4.

Row 34: P8, k3, p15, k3, p7.

Row 35: K7, p3, k15, p3, k8.

Row 36 and 37: Rep Rows 34 and 35.

Row 38: P8, k3, p15, k3, p7.

Row 39: K6, p5, k13, p5, k7.

Row 40: P6, k7, p11, k7, p5.

Row 41: K6, p5, k13, p5, k7.

Row 42: P8, k3, p15, k3, p7.

Row 43: K7, p3, k15, p3, k8.

Row 44: P1, k1, p5, k5, p5, k1, p1, k1, p5, k5, p5, k1.

Row 45: P2, k2, p9, k2, p2, k1, p2, k2, p9, k2, p2, k1.

Row 46: [P1, k8] four times.

Row 47: [P8, k1] four times.

Row 48: [P1, k8] four times**.

To join below small leaf patterns:

Rows 1 to 45: Work as Rows 1 to 45 above.

Row 46: [P1, k17] twice.

Row 47: P5, k1, p23, k1, p5, k1.

Row 48: P1, k5, [p1, k11] twice, p1, k5.

Individual squares

Cast on 36 sts.

Work from * to **.

Cast (bind) off.

To join below small leaf patterns:

	1	2	3	4	5	6	7	8	9	10	11	12	13	14	15	16	17	18	19	20	21	22	23	24	25	26	27	28	29	30	31	32	33	34	35	36	
48	x	x	5	x	x		x	x	x	x	x	x	11	x	x	x	x	x		x	x	x	x	x	11	x	x	x	x	x		x	x	5	x	x	48
47	x	x	5	x	x		x	x	x	x	x	x	x	x	x	x	x	x		x	x	x	x	x	23	x	x	x	x		x	x	x	5	x	x	47
46	x	x	x	x	x	x	x	x	x	x	x	x	17	x	x	x	x	x		x	x	x	x	x	17	x	x	x	x	x	x	x	x	x	x	x	46

To join to large or medium leaf patterns:

	1	2	3	4	5	6	7	8	9	10	11	12	13	14	15	16	17	18	19	20	21	22	23	24	25	26	27	28	29	30	31	32	33	34	35	36	
48	x	x	x	8	x	x	x	x	x		x	x	x	8	x	x	x	x		x	x	x	8	x	x	x	x		x	x	x	8	x	x	x	x	48
47	x	x	x	8	x	x	x	x			x	x	x	8	x	x	x	x		x	x	x	8	x	x	x	x		x	x	x	8	x	x	x	x	47
46	x	x	x	8	x	x	x	x			x	x	x	8	x	x	x	x		x	x	x	8	x	x	x	x		x	x	x	8	x	x	x	x	46
45		x	x			x	x	x	x	9	x	x	x	x	x			x	x		x	x			x	x	x	x	9	x	x	x	x			x	45
44		x			5			x	x	5	x	x			5				x		x			5			x	x	5	x	x			5		x	44
43	8								x	x	x								15								x	x	x					7			43
42	8								x	x	x								15								x	x	x					7			42
41	7							x	x	5	x	x							13							x	x	5	x	x				6			41
40	6						x	x	x	7	x	x	x						11						x	x	x	7	x	x	x			5			40
39	7							x	x	5	x	x							13							x	x	5	x	x				6			39
38	8								x	x	x								15								x	x	x					7			38
37	8								x	x	x								15								x	x	x					7			37
36	8								x	x	x								15								x	x	x					7			36
35	8								x	x	x								15								x	x	x					7			35
34	8								x	x	x								15								x	x	x					7			34
33	4				x						x	x	x			x			7				x				x	x	x				x				33
32	4				x	x			x	x	x	x			x	x			7			x	x				x	x	x			x	x				32
31	4				x	x	x		x	x	x			x	x	x			7			x	x	x			x	x	x		x	x	x				31
30	4				x	x	x	x	x	11	x	x	x	x	x				7			x	x	x	x	x	11	x	x	x	x	x					30
29			x	x	x	x	x	x	x	13	x	x	x	x	x	x	x		5			x	x	x	x	x	13	x	x	x	x	x	x	x			29
28			x	x	x	x	x	x	x	13	x	x	x	x	x	x	x		5			x	x	x	x	x	13	x	x	x	x	x	x	x			28
27				x	x	x	x	x	x	13	x	x	x	x	x	x	x		5			x	x	x	x	x	13	x	x	x	x	x	x	x			27
26		x	x	x	x	x	x	x	x	15	x	x	x	x	x	x	x	x		x	x	x	x		x	x	15	x	x	x	x	x	x	x	x		26
25		x	x	x	7	x	x	x	x			x	x	x	x	7	x	x			x	x	7	x	x	x	x	x	x	x	x	7	x	x	x		25
24		x	x	x	7	x	x	x			x	x	x	7	x	x	x	x		x	x	7	x	x	x	x			x	x	x	7	x	x	x	x	24
23	x	x	x	x	8	x	x	x				x	x	x	x	x	x	x	15	x	x	x	x	x	x	x			x	x	x	7	x	x	x	x	23
22	x	x	x	x	7	x	x			5				x	x	x	x	x	13	x	x	x	x	x	x			5			x	x	6	x	x	x	22
21	x	x	x	x	7	x	x			5				x	x	x	x	x	13	x	x	x	x	x	x			5			x	x	6	x	x	x	21
20	x	x	x	x	7	x	x			5				x	x	x	x	x	13	x	x	x	x	x	x			5			x	x	6	x	x	x	20
19	x	x	x	x	6	x				7				x	x	x	x	x	11	x	x	x	x	x				7			x	5	x	x	x	x	19
18	x	x			x	x	x			7				x	x	x	x		x	x	x		x	x	x			7			x	x	x			x	18
17	x	x			x	x				7				x	x	x			x	x	x		x	x				7			x	x				x	17
16	x	x				x				7				x					x	x	x		x					7			x					x	16
15	x	x								15									x	x	x							15								x	15
14	x	x								15									x	x	x							15								x	14
13	x	x								15									x	x	x							15								x	13
12	x	x								15									x	x	x							15								x	12
11	x	x								15									x	x	x							15								x	11
10	x	x	x							13							x	x	5	x	x							13							x	x	10
9	x	4	x	x						11						x	x	x	7	x	x	x						11					x	x	x	x	9
8	x	x	x							13							x	x	5	x	x							13							x	x	8
7	x	x								15								x	x	x								15								x	7
6	x	x								15								x	x	x								15								x	6
5	x	x	x				5				x			5				x	x	5	x	x				5			x			x		5	x	x	5
4	x	x	5	x	x			x	x			x	x	x	x	x	x	x	9	x	x	x	x	x			x	x			x	x		x	x	4
3		x	x	x	8	x	x	x	x			x	x	x	8	x	x	x	x		x	x	x	8	x	x	x	x		x	x	x	8	x	x	x	3
2	x	x	x	x	8	x	x	x	x			x	x	x	8	x	x	x	x		x	x	x	8	x	x	x	x		x	x	x	8	x	x	x	2
1		x	x	x	8	x	x	x	x			x	x	x	8	x	x	x	x		x	x	x	8	x	x	x	x		x	x	x	8	x	x	x	1
	36	35	34	33	32	31	30	29	28	27	26	25	24	23	22	21	20	19	18	17	16	15	14	13	12	11	10	9	8	7	6	5	4	3	2	1	

MEDIUM MAPLE LEAVES

The samara, or fruit, of maple trees have varying angles of the wings across different types of maples. The samara incorporated into this square, between the medium size maple leaves, are based on a sycamore, the seeds of which I would play 'helicopters' with as a child.

One-piece blanket

Repeat each row across the blanket as many times as required for the size you are making. Note: if you have a hard colour change against the previous square, knit across Row 1 for a neater join, instead of working the pattern row.

To join to large or medium leaf patterns:
*Row 1: [P8, k1] four times.
Row 2: [P1, k8] four times.
Row 3: [P8, k1] four times.
Row 4: K5, p2, k2, p1, k2, p2, k9, p2, k2, p1, k2, p2, k4.
Row 5: P2, k5, p1, k1, p1, k5, p5, k5, p1, k1, p1, k5, p3.
Row 6: K3, p13, k5, p13, k2.
Row 7: P3, k11, p7, k11, p4.
Row 8: K5, p9, k9, p9, k4.
Row 9: P3, k11, p7, k11, p4.
Row 10: K3, p13, k5, p13, k2.
Row 11: P2, k13, p5, k13, p3.
Rows 12 and 13: Rep Rows 10 and 11.
Row 14: K3, p3, k1, p5, k1, p3, k5, p3, k1, p5, k1, p3, k2.
Row 15: P2, k2, p2, k5, p2, k2, p5, k2, p2, k5, p2, k2, p3.
Row 16: K3, p1, k3, p5, k3, p1, k5, p1, k3, p5, k3, p1, k2.
Row 17: P6, k5, p13, k5, p7.
Row 18: K7, p5, k13, p5, k6.
Row 19: P7, k3, p15, k3, p8.
Row 20: K8, p3, k15, p3, k7.
Row 21: P3, k2, p3, k1, p3, k2, p7, k2, p3, k1, p3, k2, p4.

Row 22: K3, [p4, k5] three times, p4, k2.
Row 23: P2, [k4, p5] three times, k4, p3.
Row 24: [K3, p5] twice, k5, p5, k3, p5, k2.
Row 25: [P3, k4] twice, p7, k4, p3, k4, p4.
Row 26: K5, p3, k3, p3, k9, p3, k3, p3, k4.
Row 27: P5, [k1, p1] three times, k1, p11, [k1, p1] three times, k1, p6.
Row 28: [P1, k6, p5, k6] twice.
Row 29: K1, p5, k5, p5, k3, p5, k5, p5, k2.
Row 30: P2, k5, p5, k5, p3, k5, p5, k5, p1.
Row 31: K2, p6, k1, p6, k5, p6, k1, p6, k3.
Row 32: P3, k6, p1, k6, p5, k6, p1, k6, p2.
Row 33: K2, p3, [k1, p2] twice, k1, p3, k5, p3, [k1, p2] twice, k1, p3, k3.
Row 34: P3, k2, p2, k2, p1, k2, p2, k2, p5, k2, p2, k2, p1, [k2, p2] twice.
Row 35: K2, p1, k3, p5, k3, p1, k5, p1, k3, p5, k3, p1, k3.
Row 36: P7, k5, p13, k5, p6.
Row 37: K6, p5, k13, p5, k7.
Rows 38 and 39: Rep Rows 36 and 37.
Row 40: P6, k7, p11, k7, p5.
Row 41: K4, p9, k9, p9, k5.
Row 42: P6, k7, p11, k7, p5.
Row 43: K6, p5, k13, p5, k7.
Row 44: P1, k1, p5, k5, p5, k1, p1, k1, p5, k5, p5, k1.

Row 45: P2, k2, p9, k2, p2, k1, p2, k2, p9, k2, p2, k1.
Row 46: [P1, k8] four times.
Row 47: [P8, k1] four times.
Row 48: [P1, k8] four times**.

To join below small leaf patterns:
Rows 1 to 45: Work as Rows 1 to 45 above.
Row 46: [P1, k17] twice.
Row 47: P5, k1, p23, k1, p5, k1.
Row 48: P1, k5, [p1, k11] twice, p1, k5.

Individual squares

Cast on 36 sts.

Work from * to **.

Cast (bind) off.

To join below small leaf patterns:

	1	2	3	4	5	6	7	8	9	10	11	12	13	14	15	16	17	18	19	20	21	22	23	24	25	26	27	28	29	30	31	32	33	34	35	36	
48		x	x	5	x	x			x	x	x	x	x	x	11	x	x	x	x	x		x	x	x	x	x	11	x	x	x	x		x	x	5	x	x	48
47		x	x	5	x	x			x	x	x	x	x	x		x	x	x	x	x		x	x	x	x	x	23	x	x	x	x		x	x	5	x	x	47
46		x	x	x	x	x	x	x		x	x	x	x	17	x	x	x	x	x		x	x	x	x	x	17	x	x	x	x	x		x	x	x	x	x	46

To join to large or medium leaf patterns:

	1	2	3	4	5	6	7	8	9	10	11	12	13	14	15	16	17	18	19	20	21	22	23	24	25	26	27	28	29	30	31	32	33	34	35	36	
48		x	x	x	x	8	x	x	x		x	x	x	x	8	x	x	x		x	x	x	x	8	x	x	x		x	x	x	x	8	x	x	x	48
47		x	x	x	x	8	x	x	x		x	x	x	x	8	x	x	x		x	x	x	x	8	x	x	x		x	x	x	x	8	x	x	x	47
46		x	x	x	x	8	x	x	x		x	x	x	x	8	x	x	x		x	x	x	x	8	x	x	x		x	x	x	x	8	x	x	x	46
45		x	x				x	x	x	9	x	x	x	x			x	x		x	x				x	x	x	9	x	x	x					x	x	45
44		x			5			x	x	5	x	x			5			x		x			5		x	x	5	x	x			5				x	44
43				7				x	x	5	x	x						13						x	x	5	x	x						6			43
42				6			x	x	x	7	x	x	x					11					x	x	x	7	x	x	x					5			42
41				5		x	x	x	x	9	x	x	x	x				9				x	x	x	x	9	x	x	x	x				4			41
40				6			x	x	x	7	x	x	x					11					x	x	x	7	x	x	x					5			40
39				7				x	x	5	x	x						13						x	x	5	x	x						6			39
38				7				x	x	5	x	x						13						x	x	5	x	x						6			38
37				7				x	x	5	x	x						13						x	x	5	x	x						6			37
36				7				x	x	5	x	x						13						x	x	5	x	x						6			36
35				x				x	x	5	x	x				x		5			x			x	x	5	x	x					x			35
34				x	x			x	x		x	x			x	x		5			x	x		x	x		x	x			x	x				34
33				x	x	x		x	x		x	x		x	x	x		5			x	x	x	x	x		x	x		x	x	x				33
32				x	6	x	x	x	x		x	x	x	x	6	x		5			x	6	x	x	x	x		x	x	x	x	6	x			32
31				x	6	x	x	x	x		x	x	x	x	6	x		5			x	6	x	x	x	x		x	x	x	x	6	x			31
30			x	x	5	x	x			5			x	x	5	x	x			x	x	5	x	x			5			x	x	5	x	x		30
29			x	x	5	x	x			5			x	x	5	x	x			x	x	5	x	x			5			x	x	5	x	x		29
28		x	x	x	6	x	x			5			x	x	6	x	x	x		x	x	x	6	x	x			5		x	x	6	x	x	x	28
27	x	6	x	x	x	x			x		x			x		x	x	x	x	11	x	x	x	x	x		x			x		x	x	5	x	x	27
26	x	5	x	x	x				x	x	x			x	x	x	x	x	9	x	x	x	x	x			x	x	x			x	4	x	x	26
25	x	4	x	x		4			x	x	x			4		x	x	x	7	x	x		4			x	x	x			4		x		x	25
24	x	x	x			5			x	x	x			5		x	x	x	5	x	x		5			x	x	x			5			x	x	24
23	x	x	x			4		x	x	5	x	x			4		x	x	5	x	x		4		x	x	5	x	x			4			x	x	23
22	x	x	x			4		x	x	5	x	x			4		x	x	5	x	x		4		x	x	5	x	x			4			x	x	22
21	x	4	x	x				x	x	x			x	x	x			7	x	x	x			x	x	x		x	x	x				x	x	21
20	x	x	x	x	8	x	x	x			x	x	x	x	x	x	x	15	x	x	x	x	x	x	x			x	x	x	x	7	x	x	x	20
19	x	x	x	x	8	x	x	x			x	x	x	x	x	x	x	15	x	x	x	x	x	x	x			x	x	x	x	7	x	x	x	19
18	x	x	x	x	7	x	x			5			x	x	x	x	x	13	x	x	x	x	x	x			5		x	x	x	6	x	x	x	18
17	x	x	x	x	7	x	x			5			x	x	x	x	x	13	x	x	x	x	x	x			5		x	x	x	6	x	x	x	17
16	x	x	x				x	x		5			x	x	x		x	5	x	x			x	x	x		5		x	x	x		x	x	x	16
15	x	x	x			x	x			5			x	x			x	5	x	x			x	x		5			x	x			x	x	x	15
14	x	x	x				x			5			x				x	5	x	x			x			5			x				x	x	x	14
13	x	x	x							13			x	x	5	x	x			13							13							x	x	13
12	x	x	x							13			x	x	5	x	x			13							13							x	x	12
11	x	x	x							13			x	x	5	x	x			13							13							x	x	11
10	x	x	x							13			x	x	5	x	x			13							13							x	x	10
9	x	4	x	x						11			x	x	x		x	7	x	x	x						11						x	x	x	9
8	x	5	x	x	x					9			x	x	x	x	x	9	x	x	x	x					9				x	x	4	x	x	8
7	x	4	x	x						11			x	x	x		x	7	x	x	x						11						x	x	x	7
6	x	x	x							13			x	x	x		x	5	x	x							13						x	x	x	6
5	x	x	x			5			x		x		5			x	x	5	x	x		5			x		x		5			x	x	x		5
4	x	x	5	x	x			x	x		x	x			x	x	x	9	x	x	x			x	x		x	x			x	x	4	x	x	4
3		x	x	x	8	x	x	x		x	x	x	8	x	x	x		x	x	x	x	8	x	x	x		x	x	x	x	8	x	x	x		3
2		x	x	x	8	x	x	x		x	x	x	8	x	x	x		x	x	x	x	8	x	x	x		x	x	x	x	8	x	x	x		2
1		x	x	x	8	x	x	x		x	x	x	8	x	x	x		x	x	x	x	8	x	x	x		x	x	x	x	8	x	x	x		1
	36	35	34	33	32	31	30	29	28	27	26	25	24	23	22	21	20	19	18	17	16	15	14	13	12	11	10	9	8	7	6	5	4	3	2	1	

Small Maple Leaves follows the design of Large Maple Leaves, only smaller in size due to perspective from the ground. If you want to join these above Medium or Large Maple Leaves, you will need the alternative instructions here and for the large or medium leaf you wish to join it to.

One-piece blanket

Repeat each row across the blanket as many times as required for the size you are making. Note: if you have a hard colour change against the previous square, knit across Row 1 for a neater join, instead of working the pattern row.

To join to small leaf patterns:
***Row 1**: [P5, k1] six times.
Row 2: [P1, k2, p2, k1, p1, k1, p2, k2] three times.
Row 3: [P1, k9, p1, k1] three times.
Row 4: K2, [p9, k3] twice, p9, k1.
Row 5: P1, [k9, p3] twice, k9, p2.
Row 6: K3, [p7, k5] twice, p7, k2.
Row 7: P1, [k9, p3] twice, k9, p2.
Rows 8 and 9: Rep Rows 4 and 5.
Row 10: K2, [p2, k1, p3, k1, p2, k3] twice, p2, k1, p3, k1, p2, k1.
Row 11: P1, [k1, p2, k3, p2, k1, p3] twice, k1, p2, k3, p2, k1, p2.
Row 12: [P1, k4, p3, k4] three times.
Row 13: K1, [p3, k3] five times, p3, k2.
Row 14: P2, [k4, p1, k4, p3] twice, [k4, p1] twice.
Row 15: K1, p2, k1, [p3, k1, p2, k3, p2, k1] twice, p3, k1, p2, k2.
Row 16: P2, k1, p2, [k3, p2, k1, p3, k1, p2] twice, k3, p2, k1, p1.

Row 17: K4, [p3, k9] twice, p3, k5.
Row 18: P5, [k3, p9] twice, k3, p4.
Row 19: K4, [p3, k9] twice, p3, k5.
Row 20: P4, [k5, p7] twice, k5, p3.
Row 21: K4, [p3, k9] twice, p3, k5.
Row 22: P5, [k3, p9] twice, k3, p4.
Row 23: K4, [p1, k1, p1, k9] twice, p1, k1, p1, k5.
Row 24: P1, k1, p2, [k2, p1, k2, p2, k1, p1, k1, p2] twice, k2, p1, k2, p2, k1.
Rows 25 to 48: Rep Rows 1 to 24**.

To join above large or medium leaf patterns:
Row 1: P5, [k1, p11] twice, k1, p5, k1.
Row 2: P1, k2, p2, k1, p1, k1, p2, [k5, p2, k1, p1, k1, p2] twice, k2.
Row 3: P1, [k9, p3] twice, k9, p1, k1.
Rows 4 to 48: Work as Rows 4 to 48 above (working Rows 1 to 3 as above for Rows 25 to 27).

Individual squares

Cast on 36 sts.
Work from * to **.
Cast (bind) off.

To join to small leaf patterns:

Columns (top): 1 2 3 4 5 6 7 8 9 10 11 12 13 14 15 16 17 18 19 20 21 22 23 24 25 26 27 28 29 30 31 32 33 34 35 36

[Colorwork / knitting chart grid, 48 rows numbered on both sides. Selected cells contain "x" marks or number symbols. Notable numbered cells by row:]

Row 23: 5 (col 2), 9 (col 13), 9 (col 23), 4 (col 34)
Row 22: 5 (col 2), 9 (col 13), 9 (col 23), 4 (col 34)
Row 21: 5 (col 2), 9 (col 13), 9 (col 23), 4 (col 34)
Row 20: 4 (col 2), 5 (col 8), 7 (col 13), 5 (col 19), 7 (col 23), 5 (col 28)
Row 19: 5 (col 2), 9 (col 13), 9 (col 23), 4 (col 34)
Row 18: 5 (col 2), 9 (col 13), 9 (col 23), 4 (col 34)
Row 17: 5 (col 2), 9 (col 13), 9 (col 23), 4 (col 34)
Row 14: 4 (cols), x marks
Row 12: 4 marks
Row 9: 9 (col 6), 9 (col 19), 9 (col 29)
Row 8: 9 (col 6), 9 (col 19), 9 (col 29)
Row 7: 9 (col 6), 9 (col 19), 9 (col 29)
Row 6: 7 (col 6), 5 (col 10), 7 (col 19), 5 (col 23), 7 (col 29)
Row 5: 9 (col 6), 9 (col 19), 9 (col 29)
Row 4: 9 (col 6), 9 (col 19), 9 (col 29)
Row 3: 9 (col 6), 9 (col 19), 9 (col 29)
Row 1: x x 5 x x ... 5 ... 5 ... 5 ... (repeating)

Columns (bottom): 36 35 34 33 32 31 30 29 28 27 26 25 24 23 22 21 20 19 18 17 16 15 14 13 12 11 10 9 8 7 6 5 4 3 2 1

To join above large or medium leaf patterns:

Row											
3	x	9				9				x	x
2	x x	x	x	x x 5 x x	x	x	x x 5 x x	x	x x	
1	x x 5 x x	x x x x x x 11 x x x x x x	x x 5 x x x	11 x x x x x	x x 5 x x						

Columns (bottom): 36 35 34 33 32 31 30 29 28 27 26 25 24 23 22 21 20 19 18 17 16 15 14 13 12 11 10 9 8 7 6 5 4 3 2 1

26 / OAK TREE TRUNKS

One-piece blanket

Repeat each row across the blanket as many times as required for the size you are making. Note: if you have a hard colour change against the previous square, knit across Row 1 for a neater join, instead of working the pattern row.

*Row 1: P3, [k3, p1] twice, k3, p7, [k3, p1] twice, k3, p4.
Row 2: K4, [p3, k1] twice, p3, k7, [p3, k1] twice, p3, k3.
Rows 3 and 4: Rep Rows 1 and 2.
Row 5: P3, k1, [p1, k3] twice, p1, k1, p7, k1, [p1, k3] twice, p1, k1, p4.
Row 6: K4, p1, [k1, p3] twice, k1, p1, k7, p1, [k1, p3] twice, k1, p1, k3.
Rows 7 and 8: Rep Rows 5 and 6.
Rows 9 to 48: Rep Rows 1 to 8 five times more**.

Individual squares

Cast on 36 sts.

Work from * to **.

Cast (bind) off.

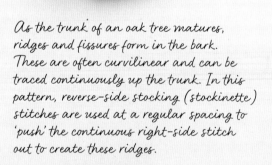

As the trunk of an oak tree matures, ridges and fissures form in the bark. These are often curvilinear and can be traced continuously up the trunk. In this pattern, reverse-side stocking (stockinette) stitches are used at a regular spacing to 'push' the continuous right-side stitch out to create these ridges.

	1	2	3	4	5	6	7	8	9	10	11	12	13	14	15	16	17	18	19	20	21	22	23	24	25	26	27	28	29	30	31	32	33	34	35	36	
48	x	x	x	x		x				x				x		x	x	x	x	x	x	x		x				x				x		x	x	x	48
47	x	x	x	x		x				x				x		x	x	x	x	x	x	x		x				x				x		x	x	x	47
46	x	x	x	x		x				x				x		x	x	x	x	x	x	x		x				x				x		x	x	x	46
45	x	x	x	x		x				x				x		x	x	x	x	x	x	x		x				x				x		x	x	x	45
44	x	x	x	x				x				x				x	x	x	x	x	x	x				x				x				x	x	x	44
43	x	x	x	x				x				x				x	x	x	x	x	x	x				x				x				x	x	x	43
42	x	x	x	x				x				x				x	x	x	x	x	x	x				x				x				x	x	x	42
41	x	x	x	x				x				x				x	x	x	x	x	x	x				x				x				x	x	x	41
40	x	x	x	x		x				x				x		x	x	x	x	x	x	x		x				x				x		x	x	x	40
39	x	x	x	x		x				x				x		x	x	x	x	x	x	x		x				x				x		x	x	x	39
38	x	x	x	x		x				x				x		x	x	x	x	x	x	x		x				x				x		x	x	x	38
37	x	x	x	x		x				x				x		x	x	x	x	x	x	x		x				x				x		x	x	x	37
36	x	x	x	x				x				x				x	x	x	x	x	x	x				x				x				x	x	x	36
35	x	x	x	x				x				x				x	x	x	x	x	x	x				x				x				x	x	x	35
34	x	x	x	x				x				x				x	x	x	x	x	x	x				x				x				x	x	x	34
33	x	x	x	x				x				x				x	x	x	x	x	x	x				x				x				x	x	x	33
32	x	x	x	x		x				x				x		x	x	x	x	x	x	x		x				x				x		x	x	x	32
31	x	x	x	x		x				x				x		x	x	x	x	x	x	x		x				x				x		x	x	x	31
30	x	x	x	x		x				x				x		x	x	x	x	x	x	x		x				x				x		x	x	x	30
29	x	x	x	x		x				x				x		x	x	x	x	x	x	x		x				x				x		x	x	x	29
28	x	x	x	x				x				x				x	x	x	x	x	x	x				x				x				x	x	x	28
27	x	x	x	x				x				x				x	x	x	x	x	x	x				x				x				x	x	x	27
26	x	x	x	x				x				x				x	x	x	x	x	x	x				x				x				x	x	x	26
25	x	x	x	x				x				x				x	x	x	x	x	x	x				x				x				x	x	x	25
24	x	x	x	x		x				x				x		x	x	x	x	x	x	x		x				x				x		x	x	x	24
23	x	x	x	x		x				x				x		x	x	x	x	x	x	x		x				x				x		x	x	x	23
22	x	x	x	x		x				x				x		x	x	x	x	x	x	x		x				x				x		x	x	x	22
21	x	x	x	x		x				x				x		x	x	x	x	x	x	x		x				x				x		x	x	x	21
20	x	x	x	x				x				x				x	x	x	x	x	x	x				x				x				x	x	x	20
19	x	x	x	x				x				x				x	x	x	x	x	x	x				x				x				x	x	x	19
18	x	x	x	x				x				x				x	x	x	x	x	x	x				x				x				x	x	x	18
17	x	x	x	x				x				x				x	x	x	x	x	x	x				x				x				x	x	x	17
16	x	x	x	x		x				x				x		x	x	x	x	x	x	x		x				x				x		x	x	x	16
15	x	x	x	x		x				x				x		x	x	x	x	x	x	x		x				x				x		x	x	x	15
14	x	x	x	x		x				x				x		x	x	x	x	x	x	x		x				x				x		x	x	x	14
13	x	x	x	x		x				x				x		x	x	x	x	x	x	x		x				x				x		x	x	x	13
12	x	x	x	x				x				x				x	x	x	x	x	x	x				x				x				x	x	x	12
11	x	x	x	x				x				x				x	x	x	x	x	x	x				x				x				x	x	x	11
10	x	x	x	x				x				x				x	x	x	x	x	x	x				x				x				x	x	x	10
9	x	x	x	x				x				x				x	x	x	x	x	x	x				x				x				x	x	x	9
8	x	4	x	x		x				x				x		x	x	x	7	x	x	x		x				x				x		x	x	x	8
7	x	4	x	x		x				x				x		x	x	x	7	x	x	x		x				x				x		x	x	x	7
6	x	4	x	x		x				x				x		x	x	x	7	x	x	x		x				x				x		x	x	x	6
5	x	4	x	x		x				x				x		x	x	x	7	x	x	x		x				x				x		x	x	x	5
4	x	4	x	x				x				x				x	x	x	7	x	x	x				x				x				x	x	x	4
3	x	4	x	x				x				x				x	x	x	7	x	x	x				x				x				x	x	x	3
2	x	4	x	x				x				x				x	x	x	7	x	x	x				x				x				x	x	x	2
1	x	4	x	x				x				x				x	x	x	7	x	x	x				x				x				x	x	x	1
	36	35	34	33	32	31	30	29	28	27	26	25	24	23	22	21	20	19	18	17	16	15	14	13	12	11	10	9	8	7	6	5	4	3	2	1	

27 / LARGE OAK LEAVES

One-piece blanket

Repeat each row across the blanket as many times as required for the size you are making. Note: if you have a hard colour change against the previous square, knit across Row 1 for a neater join, instead of working the pattern row.

To join to large or medium leaf patterns:
*Row 1: [P8, k1] four times.
Row 2: [P1, k8] four times.
Row 3: [P8, k1] four times.
Row 4: K7, p5, k13, p5, k6.
Row 5: P4, k9, p9, k9, p5.
Row 6: K5, p9, k9, p9, k4.
Row 7: P4, k9, p9, k9, p5.
Row 8: K6, p7, k11, p7, k5.
Row 9: P4, k9, p9, k9, p5.
Row 10: K4, p11, k7, p11, k3.
Row 11: P3, k11, p7, k11, p4.
Row 12: K4, p11, k7, p11, k3.
Row 13: P4, k9, p9, k9, p5.
Row 14: K4, p11, k7, p11, k3.
Row 15: P2, k13, p5, k13, p3.
Row 16: K3, p13, k5, p13, k2.
Rows 17 and 18: Rep Rows 15 and 16.
Row 19: P4, k9, p9, k9, p5.
Row 20: K5, p9, k9, p9, k4.
Row 21: P4, k9, p9, k9, p5.
Row 22: K6, p7, k11, p7, k5.
Row 23: P7, k3, p15, k3, p8.
Row 24: [P1, k7, p3, k7] twice.
Row 25: [K1, p7] twice, k3, p7, k1, p7, k2.
Row 26: P2, k15, p3, k15, p1.
Row 27: K3, p11, k7, p11, k4.
Row 28: P5, k9, p9, k9, p4.
Row 29: K4, p9, k9, p9, k5.
Row 30: P5, k9, p9, k9, p4.
Row 31: K6, p5, k13, p5, k7.
Row 32: P7, k5, p13, k5, p6.
Rows 33 and 34: Rep Rows 31 and 32.
Row 35: K5, p7, k11, p7, k6.
Row 36: P5, k9, p9, k9, p4.
Row 37: K5, p7, k11, p7, k6.
Row 38: P6, k7, p11, k7, p5.
Row 39: K5, p7, k11, p7, k6.
Row 40: P5, k9, p9, k9, p4.
Row 41: K3, p11, k7, p11, k4.
Row 42: P5, k9, p9, k9, p4.
Row 43: K4, p9, k9, p9, k5.
Row 44: P5, k9, p9, k9, p4.
Row 45: K2, p13, k5, p13, k3.
Row 46: [P1, k8] four times.
Row 47: [P8, k1] four times.
Row 48: [P1, k8] four times******.

To join below small leaf patterns:
Rows 1 to 45: Work as Rows 1 to 45 above.
Row 46: [P1, k17] twice.
Row 47: P5, k1, p23, k1, p5, k1.
Row 48: P1, k5, [p1, k11] twice, p1, k5.

Individual squares

Cast on 36 sts.

Work from * to **.

Cast (bind) off.

To join below small leaf patterns:

	1	2	3	4	5	6	7	8	9	10	11	12	13	14	15	16	17	18	19	20	21	22	23	24	25	26	27	28	29	30	31	32	33	34	35	36	
48		x	x	5	x	x			x	x	x	x	11	x	x	x	x	x	x		x	x	x	x	11	x	x	x	x	x			x	x	5	x	x	48
47		x	x	5	x	x			x	x	x	23																					x	x	5	x	x	47
46		x	x	x	x	x	x	x	x	x	x	17	x	x	x	x	x	x		x	x	x	x	x	17	x	x	x	x	x	x	x	x	x	5	x	x	46

To join to large or medium leaf patterns:

	1	2	3	4	5	6	7	8	9	10	11	12	13	14	15	16	17	18	19	20	21	22	23	24	25	26	27	28	29	30	31	32	33	34	35	36	
48		x	x	x	x	x	x	x	8	x		x	8	x	x	x	x	x	x		x	x	x	x	x	8	x		x	8	x	x	x	x	x	x	48
47		x	x	x	x	x	x	8	x		x	8	x	x	x	x	x	x		x	x	x	x	x	8	x		x	8	x	x	x	x	x			47
46		x	x	x	x	x	x	8	x		x	8	x	x	x	x	x	x		x	x	x	x	x	8	x		x	8	x	x	x	x	x			46
45			x	x	x	x	x	x		13	x	x	x	x	x	x			5			x	x	x	x	x		13	x	x	x	x					45
44		5			x	x	x	x	x	9	x	x	x	x	x			9				x	x	x	x	9	x	x	x	x				4			44
43		5			x	x	x	x	x	9	x	x	x	x	x			9				x	x	x	x	9	x	x	x	x				4			43
42		5			x	x	x	x	x	9	x	x	x	x	x			9				x	x	x	x	9	x	x	x	x				4			42
41		4			x	x	x	x	x	11	x	x	x	x	x			7			x	x	x	x	x	11	x	x	x	x	x						41
40		5			x	x	x	x	x	9	x	x	x	x	x			9			x	x	x	x	x	9	x	x	x	x				4			40
39		6				x	x	x	x	7	x	x	x				11			x	x	x	7	x	x	x					5					39
38		6				x	x	x	x	7	x	x	x				11			x	x	x	7	x	x	x					5					38
37		6				x	x	x	x	7	x	x	x				11			x	x	x	7	x	x	x					5					37
36		5				x	x	x	x	9	x	x	x	x	x			9			x	x	x	x	9	x	x	x	x				4				36
35		6				x	x	x	x	7	x	x	x				11			x	x	x	7	x	x	x					5					35
34		7				x	x	x	5	x	x	x				13			x	x	x	5	x	x	x						6					34
33		7				x	x	x	5	x	x	x				13			x	x	x	5	x	x	x						6					33
32		7				x	x	x	5	x	x	x				13			x	x	x	5	x	x	x						6					32
31		7				x	x	x	5	x	x	x				13				x	x	x	5	x	x	x					6					31
30		5				x	x	x	x	9	x	x	x	x	x			9			x	x	x	x	9	x	x	x	x				4				30
29		5				x	x	x	x	9	x	x	x	x				9			x	x	x	x	9	x	x	x	x				4				29
28		5				x	x	x	x	9	x	x	x	x	x			9			x	x	x	x	9	x	x	x	x				4				28
27		4			x	x	x	x	x	11	x	x	x	x	x			7			x	x	x	x	x	11	x	x	x	x	x						27
26		x	x	x	x	x	x	x	x	15	x	x	x	x	x	x	x			x	x	x	x	x	15	x	x	x	x	x	x	x				26
25		x	x	7	x	x	x	x		x	x	x	x	x	7	x	x			x	x	7	x	x		x	x	x	x	7	x	x				25
24		x	x	x	7	x	x	x	x		x	x	x	x	x	7	x	x	x	x	x	x	7	x	x				x	x	x	7	x	x	x		24
23	x	x	x	x	x	8	x	x			x	x	x	x	x	x		15	x	x	x	x		x	x	x		x	x	x	7	x	x				23
22	x	x	6	x	x	x			7			x	x	x	x	x	11	x	x	x	x	x			7					x	x	5	x	x			22
21	x	x	5	x	x			9				x	x	x	x	9	x	x	x	x				9					x	4	x	x					21
20	x	x	5	x	x			9				x	x	x	x	9	x	x	x	x				9					x	4	x	x					20
19	x	x	5	x	x			9				x	x	x	x	9	x	x	x	x				9					x	4	x	x					19
18	x	x	x					13						x	x	5	x	x						13						x	x	x					18
17	x	x						13						x	x	5	x	x						13						x	x	x					17
16	x	x	x					13						x	x	5	x	x						13						x	x	x					16
15	x	x	x					13						x	x	5	x	x						13						x	x	x					15
14	x	x	4	x				11					x	x	x	7	x	x	x					11						x	x	x					14
13	x	x	5	x	x			9				x	x	x	x	9	x	x	x	x				9					x	4	x	x					13
12	x	x	4	x				11					x	x	x	7	x	x	x					11						x	x	x					12
11	x	x	4	x				11					x	x	x	7	x	x	x					11						x	x	x					11
10	x	x	4	x				11					x	x	x	7	x	x	x					11						x	x	x					10
9	x	x	5	x	x			9				x	x	x	x	9	x	x	x					9					x	4	x	x					9
8	x	x	6	x	x	x		7				x	x	x	x	x	11	x	x	x	x				7				x	x	5	x	x				8
7	x	x	5	x	x			9				x	x	x	x	9	x	x	x					9					x	4	x	x					7
6	x	x	5	x	x			9				x	x	x	x	9	x	x	x					9					x	4	x	x					6
5	x	x	5	x	x			9				x	x	x	x	9	x	x	x					9					x	4	x	x					5
4	x	x	7	x	x	x	x		5			x	x	x	x	x	13	x	x	x	x	x			5			x	x	x	x	6	x	x			4
3	x	8	x	x	x	x	x	x		x	x	x	x	8	x		x	8	x	x	x	x	x		x	x	x	x	x	x	8	x	x				3
2	x	8	x	x	x	x	x	x		x	x	x	x	8	x		x	8	x	x	x	x	x		x	x	x	x	x	x	8	x	x				2
1	x	8	x	x	x	x	x	x		x	x	x	x	8	x		x	8	x	x	x	x	x		x	x	x	x	x	x	8	x	x				1
	36	35	34	33	32	31	30	29	28	27	26	25	24	23	22	21	20	19	18	17	16	15	14	13	12	11	10	9	8	7	6	5	4	3	2	1	

Lobed oak leaves come in a variety of shapes and sizes, the leaves here are based on the four to five smooth lobed leaves of an English oak. The combination of horizontal and vertical elements in the lobed leaves made it difficult to maintain the texture in the pattern, so the detail has been kept to a minimum.

The acorn featured in this square is symbolic of future potential, of not giving up because something seems so small at the beginning: 'Mighty oaks from little acorns grow'. You could think of your knitting project like an acorn, starting as a small square and growing into a mighty blanket!

One-piece blanket

Repeat each row across the blanket as many times as required for the size you are making. Note: if you have a hard colour change against the previous square, knit across Row 1 for a neater join, instead of working the pattern row.

To join to large or medium leaf patterns:

*Row 1: [P8, k1] four times.
Row 2: [P1, k8] four times.
Row 3: [P8, k1] four times.
Row 4: K6, p7, k11, p7, k5.
Row 5: P5, k7, p11, k7, p6.
Row 6: K6, p7, k11, p7, k5.
Row 7: P6, k5, p13, k5, p7.
Row 8: K5, p9, k9, p9, k4.
Row 9: P4, k9, p9, k9, p5.
Row 10: K5, p9, k9, p9, k4.
Row 11: P5, k7, p11, k7, p6.
Row 12: K5, p9, k9, p9, k4.
Row 13: P3, k11, p7, k11, p4.
Row 14: K4, p11, k7, p11, k3.
Row 15: P3, k11, p7, k11, p4.
Row 16: K6, p7, k11, p7, k5.
Row 17: P5, k7, p11, k7, p6.
Row 18: K6, p7, k11, p7, k5.
Row 19: P3, k1, p3, k3, p3, k1, p7, k1, p3, k3, p3, k1, p4.
Row 20: K3, [p3, k2] twice, p3, k5, [p3, k2] three times.
Row 21: P1, k5, p2, k1, p2, k5, p3, k5, p2, k1, p2, k5, p2.
Row 22: K2, p5, k5, p5, k3, p5, k5, p5, k1.
Row 23: P1, k5, p5, k5, p3, k5, p5, k5, p2.

Row 24: K3, p1, k1, p1, k7, p1, k1, p1, k5, p1, k1, p1, k7, p1, k1, p1, k2.
Row 25: [P1, k1] three times, p5, [k1, p1] twice, k1, p3, [k1, p1] twice, k1, p5, [k1, p1] twice, k1, p2.
Row 26: K3, p1, k1, p1, k7, p1, k1, p1, k5, p1, k1, p1, k7, p1, k1, p1, k2.
Row 27: P3, [k1, p4] twice, k1, p7, [k1, p4] three times.
Row 28: [P1, k3] twice, p3, k3, [p1, k3] three times, p3, k3, p1, k3.
Row 29: [K1, p2] twice, k5, p2, k1, p2, k3, p2, k1, p2, k5, p2, k1, p2, k2.
Row 30: P2, k5, p5, k5, p3, k5, p5, k5, p1.
Row 31: K3, p3, k5, p3, k7, p3, k5, p3, k4.
Row 32: P4, k4, p1, k1, p1, k4, p7, k4, p1, k1, p1, k4, p3.
Row 33: K3, p3, [k1, p1] twice, k1, p3, k7, p3, [k1, p1] twice, k1, p3, k4.
Row 34: P6, k2, p1, k1, p1, k2, p11, k2, p1, k1, p1, k2, p5.
Row 35: K5, p3, k1, p3, k11, p3, k1, p3, k6.
Row 36: P6, k3, p1, k3, p11, k3, p1, k3, p5.
Row 37: K4, p4, k1, p4, k9, p4, k1, p4, k5.
Row 38: P4, k11, p7, k11, p3.
Row 39: K4, p9, k9, p9, k5.
Row 40: P5, k9, p9, k9, p4.
Row 41: K4, p9, k9, p9, k5.
Row 42: P3, k13, p5, k13, p2.
Row 43: K3, p11, k7, p11, k4.
Row 44: P4, k11, p7, k11, p3.

Row 45: K3, p11, k7, p11, k4.
Row 46: [P1, k8] four times.
Row 47: [P8, k1] four times.
Row 48: [P1, k8] four times**.

To join below small leaf patterns:

Rows 1 to 45: Work as Rows 1 to 45 above.
Row 46: [P1, k17] twice.
Row 47: P5, k1, p23, k1, p5, k1.
Row 48: P1, k5, [p1, k11] twice, p1, k5.

Individual squares

Cast on 36 sts.

Work from * to **.

Cast (bind) off.

	1	2	3	4	5	6	7	8	9	10	11	12	13	14	15	16	17	18	19	20	21	22	23	24	25	26	27	28	29	30	31	32	33	34	35	36	
48		x	x	5	x	x			x	x	x	x	x	11	x	x	x	x	x		x	x	x	x	x	11	x	x	x	x	x		x	5	x	x	48
47		x	x	5	x	x			x	x	x	x	x	x	x	x	x	x	x	x	x	x	x	x	23	x	x	x	x	x		x	5	x	x	47
46		x	x	x	x	x			x	x	x	x	x	17	x	x	x	x	x		x	x	x	x	x	17	x	x	x	x	x		x	x	x	x	46

To join to large or medium leaf patterns:

	1	2	3	4	5	6	7	8	9	10	11	12	13	14	15	16	17	18	19	20	21	22	23	24	25	26	27	28	29	30	31	32	33	34	35	36	
48		x	x	x	x	x	x	8	x		x	8	x	x	x	x	x	x		x	8	x	x	x	x	x	x		x	x	x	x	x	x	8	x	48
47		x	x	x	x	x	x	8	x		x	8	x	x	x	x	x	x		x	8	x	x	x	x	x	x		x	x	x	x	x	x	8	x	47
46		x	x	x	x	x	x	8	x		x	8	x	x	x	x	x	x		x	8	x	x	x	x	x	x		x	x	x	x	x	x	8	x	46
45		4			x	x	x	x	x	11	x	x	x	x	x			7			x	x	x	x	x	11	x	x	x	x	x						45
44		4		x	x	x	x	x	x	11	x	x	x	x	x			7		x	x	x	x	x	11	x	x	x	x	x						44
43		4		x	x	x	x	x	x	11	x	x	x	x	x			7		x	x	x	x	x	11	x	x	x	x	x						43
42			x	x	x	x	x	x	x	13	x	x	x	x	x	x		5		x	x	x	x	x	13	x	x	x	x	x	x					42
41		5			x	x	x	x	x	9	x	x	x	x			9			x	x	x	x	9	x	x	x	x			4					41
40		5		x	x	x	x	x	x	9	x	x	x	x			9		x	x	x	x	x	9	x	x	x	x			4					40
39		5		x	x	x	x	x	x	9	x	x	x	x			9		x	x	x	x	x	9	x	x	x	x			4					39
38		4		x	x	x	x	x	x	11	x	x	x	x	x			7		x	x	x	x	x	11	x	x	x	x	x						38
37		5			x	x	4	x		x	4	x	x			9			x	x	4	x		x	4	x	x			4					37
36		6			x	x	x		x	x	x			11				x	x	x		x	x	x				5							36
35		6			x	x	x		x	x	x			11				x	x	x		x	x	x				5							35
34		6			x	x	x		x	x	x			11				x	x	x		x	x	x				5							34
33		4		x	x	x		x			x	x	x			7			x	x	x		x			x	x	x							33
32		4		x	x	4	x		x		x	4	x	x			7		x	x	4	x		x		x	4	x	x						32
31		4		x	x	x			5		x	x	x			7			x	x	x			5		x	x	x							31
30		x	x	5	x	x		5		x	x	5	x	x			x	x	5	x	x		5		x	x	5	x	x					30
29		x	x		x	x		5		x	x		x	x			x	x		x	x		5		x	x		x	x					29
28		x	x	x	x	x		x	x	x		x	x	x	x	x	x	x		x	x	x		x	x	x	x	x		x	x	x	28
27	x	x	4	x		x	4	x	x		x	x	4	x		x	x	x	7	x	x	x		x	4	x	x		x	4	x		x	x	x	27
26	x	x	x		x		x	x	x	7	x	x	x		x		x	x	x	5	x	x		x		x	x	x	7	x	x		x		x	26
25	x	x		x		x	x	x	5	x	x		x		x	x	x	x		5	x	x		x		x	x		x	x		x	25
24	x	x	x		x		x	x	x	7	x	x	x		x	x	x	x		5	x	x		x		x	x	x	7	x	x	x	24
23	x	x		5		x	x	5	x	x		5		x	x	x		5		x	x	5	x	x		5		x	23
22	x	x		5		x	x	5	x	x		5		x	x	x		5		x	x	5	x	x		5		x	22
21	x	x		5		x	x			x	x		5		x	x	x		5		x	x			x	x		5		x	21
20	x	x	x		x	x		x	x		x	x	5	x	x		x	x	x		x	x		x	x	20
19	x	x	4	x		x	x	x		x	x	x	7	x	x	x		x	x	x		x	x	x	x	x	19
18	x	x	6	x	x	x			7		x	x	x	x	x	11	x	x	x	x	x		7		x	x	x	x	5	x	18
17	x	x	6	x	x	x			7		x	x	x	x	x	11	x	x	x	x	x		7		x	x	x	x	5	x	17
16	x	x	6	x	x	x			7		x	x	x	x	x	11	x	x	x	x	x		7		x	x	x	x	5	x	16
15	x	x	4	x			11			x	x	x	7	x	x	x		11		x	x	x	15
14	x	x	4	x			11			x	x	x	7	x	x	x		11		x	x	x	14
13	x	x	4	x			11			x	x	x	7	x	x	x		11		x	x	x	13
12	x	x	5	x	x		9		x	x	x	x	9	x	x	x	x		9		x	x	4	x	12
11	x	x	6	x	x	x		7		x	x	x	x	11	x	x	x	x		7		x	x	x	5	x	11
10	x	x	5	x	x		9		x	x	x	x	9	x	x	x	x		9		x	x	4	x	10
9	x	x	5	x	x		9		x	x	x	x	9	x	x	x	x		9		x	x	4	x	9
8	x	x	5	x	x		9		x	x	x	x	9	x	x	x	x		9		x	x	4	x	8
7	x	x	7	x	x	x	x		5		x	x	x	x	13	x	x	x	x	x		5		x	x	x	x	x	6	x	7
6	x	x	6	x	x	x		7		x	x	x	x	11	x	x	x	x	x		7		x	x	x	x	5	x	6
5	x	x	6	x	x	x		7		x	x	x	x	11	x	x	x	x	x		7		x	x	x	x	5	x	5
4	x	x	6	x	x	x		7		x	x	x	x	11	x	x	x	x	x		7		x	x	x	x	5	x	4
3		x	8	x	x	x	x	x		x	x	x	x	x	8	x		x	8	x	x	x	x	x		x	x	x	x	x	8	x	3
2		x	8	x	x	x	x	x		x	x	x	x	x	8	x		x	8	x	x	x	x	x		x	x	x	x	x	8	x	2
1		x	8	x	x	x	x	x		x	x	x	x	x	8	x		x	8	x	x	x	x	x		x	x	x	x	x	8	x	1

| 36 | 35 | 34 | 33 | 32 | 31 | 30 | 29 | 28 | 27 | 26 | 25 | 24 | 23 | 22 | 21 | 20 | 19 | 18 | 17 | 16 | 15 | 14 | 13 | 12 | 11 | 10 | 9 | 8 | 7 | 6 | 5 | 4 | 3 | 2 | 1 |

29 / SMALL OAK LEAVES

Small Oak Leaves follows the design of Large Oak Leaves, only smaller in size since you are looking up to them from the ground. If you want to join these above Medium or Large Oak Leaves, you will need the alternative instructions here and for the large or medium leaf you wish to join it to.

One-piece blanket

Repeat each row across the blanket as many times as required for the size you are making. Note: if you have a hard colour change against the previous square, knit across Row 1 for a neater join, instead of working the pattern row.

To join to small leaf patterns:
*Row 1: [P5, k1] six times.
Row 2: [P1, k3, p5, k3] three times.
Row 3: [P2, k7, p2, k1] three times.
Row 4: K3, [p7, k5] twice, p7, k2.
Row 5: P3, [k5, p7] twice, k5, p4.
Row 6: K3, [p7, k5] twice, p7, k2.
Row 7: P1, [k9, p3] twice, k9, p2.
Row 8: K2, [p9, k3] twice, p9, k1.
Row 9: P1, [k1, p1, k5, p1, k1, p3] twice, k1, p1, k5, p1, k1, p2.
Row 10: K3, [p7, k5] twice, p7, k2.
Row 11: P2, [k7, p5] twice, k7, p3.
Row 12: [P1, k4, p3, k4] three times.
Row 13: K1, [p3, k3] five times, p3, k2.
Row 14: P2, [k4, p1, k4, p3] twice, k4, p1, k4, p1.
Row 15: K3, [p5, k7] twice, p5, k4.
Row 16: P4, [k5, p7] twice, k5, p3.
Row 17: K2, [p1, k1, p3, k1, p1, k5] twice, p1, k1, p3, k1, p1, k3.

Row 18: P5, [k3, p9] twice, k3, p4.
Row 19: K4, [p3, k9] twice, p3, k5.
Row 20: P4, [k5, p7] twice, k5, p3.
Row 21: K2, [p7, k5] twice, p7, k3.
Row 22: P4, [k5, p7] twice, k5, p3.
Row 23: K3, [p2, k1, p2, k7] twice, p2, k1, p2, k4.
Row 24: P3, [k3, p1, k3, p5] twice, k3, p1, k3, p2.
Rows 25 to 48: Rep Rows 1 to 24**.

To join above large or medium leaf patterns:
Row 1: P5, [k1, p11] twice, k1, p5, k1.
Row 2: P1, k3, [p5, k7] twice, p5, k3.
Row 3: P2, [k7, p5] twice, k7, p2, k1.
Rows 4 to 48: Work as Rows 4 to 48 above (working Rows 1 to 3 as above for Rows 25 to 27).

Individual squares

Cast on 36 sts.

Work from * to **.

Cast (bind) off.

To join to small leaf patterns:

	1	2	3	4	5	6	7	8	9	10	11	12	13	14	15	16	17	18	19	20	21	22	23	24	25	26	27	28	29	30	31	32	33	34	35	36	
48				x	x	x		x	x	x						x	x	x		x	x	x						x	x	x		x	x	x			48
47					x	x		x	x								x	x		x	x								x	x		x	x				47
46					x	x	x	x	x								x	x	x	x	x								x	x	x	x	x				46
45				x	x	x	x	x	x	x						x	x	x	x	x	x	x						x	x	x	x	x	x	x			45
44					x	x	x	x	x								x	x	x	x	x								x	x	x	x	x				44
43						x	x	x										x	x	x										x	x	x					43
42						x	x	x										x	x	x										x	x	x					42
41				x		x	x	x		x						x		x	x	x		x						x		x	x	x		x			41
40					x	x	x	x	x								x	x	x	x	x								x	x	x	x	x				40
39					x	x	x	x	x								x	x	x	x	x								x	x	x	x	x				39
38			x	x	x	x		x	x	x	x				x	x	x	x		x	x	x	x				x	x	x	x		x	x	x	x		38
37			x	x	x				x	x	x				x	x	x				x	x	x				x	x	x				x	x	x		37
36		x	x	x	x				x	x	x	x		x	x	x	x				x	x	x	x		x	x	x	x				x	x	x	x	36
35	x	x	x								x	x	x	x	x								x	x	x	x	x								x	x	35
34	x	x	x								x	x	x	x	x								x	x	x	x	x								x	x	34
33	x	x		x						x		x	x	x		x						x		x	x	x		x						x		x	33
32	x	x										x	x	x										x	x	x										x	32
31	x	x										x	x	x										x	x	x										x	31
30	x	x	x								x	x	x	x	x								x	x	x	x	x								x	x	30
29	x	x	x	x						x	x	x	x	x	x	x						x	x	x	x	x	x	x						x	x	x	29
28	x	x	x								x	x	x	x	x								x	x	x	x	x								x	x	28
27		x	x								x	x		x	x								x	x		x	x								x	x	27
26		x	x	x						x	x	x		x	x	x						x	x	x		x	x	x						x	x	x	26
25		x	x	x	x	x		x	x	x	x	x		x	x	x	x	x		x	x	x	x	x		x	x	x	x	x		x	x	x	x	x	25
24				x	x	x		x	x	x			5			x	x	x		x	x	x			5			x	x	x		x	x	x			24
23		4			x	x		x	x				7				x	x		x	x				7				x	x		x	x				23
22		4			x	x	5	x	x				7				x	x	5	x	x				7				x	x	5	x	x				22
21				x	x	x	7	x	x	x			5			x	x	x	7	x	x	x			5			x	x	x	7	x	x	x			21
20		4			x	x	5	x	x				7				x	x	5	x	x				7				x	x	5	x	x				20
19		5				x	x	x					9					x	x	x					9					x	x	x			4		19
18		5				x	x	x					9					x	x	x					9					x	x	x			4		18
17				x		x	x	x		x			5			x		x	x	x		x			5			x		x	x	x		x			17
16		4			x	x	5	x	x				7				x	x	5	x	x				7				x	x	5	x	x				16
15		4			x	x	5	x	x				7				x	x	5	x	x				7				x	x	5	x	x				15
14			x	x	4	x		x	4	x	x				x	x	4	x		x	4	x	x				x	x	4	x		x	4	x	x		14
13			x	x	x				x	x	x				x	x	x				x	x	x				x	x	x				x	x	x		13
12		x	x	4	x				x	4	x	x		x	x	4	x				x	4	x	x		x	x	4	x				x	4	x	x	12
11	x	x	x				7				x	x	5	x	x				7				x	x	5	x	x				7				x	x	11
10	x	x	x				7				x	x	5	x	x				7				x	x	5	x	x				7				x	x	10
9	x	x		x			5			x		x	x	x		x			5			x		x	x	x		x			5			x		x	9
8	x	x					9					x	x	x					9					x	x	x					9					x	8
7	x	x					9					x	x	x					9					x	x	x					9					x	7
6	x	x	x				7				x	x	5	x	x				7				x	x	5	x	x				7				x	x	6
5	x	4	x	x			5			x	x	x	7	x	x	x			5			x	x	x	7	x	x	x			5			x	x	x	5
4	x	x	x				7				x	x	5	x	x				7				x	x	5	x	x				7				x	x	4
3		x	x				7				x	x		x	x				7				x	x		x	x				7				x	x	3
2		x	x	x			5			x	x	x		x	x	x			5			x	x	x		x	x	x			5			x	x	x	2
1		x	x	5	x	x		x	x	5	x	x		x	x	5	x	x		x	x	5	x	x		x	x	5	x	x		x	x	5	x	x	1
	36	35	34	33	32	31	30	29	28	27	26	25	24	23	22	21	20	19	18	17	16	15	14	13	12	11	10	9	8	7	6	5	4	3	2	1	

To join above large or medium leaf patterns:

3		x	x				7				x	x	5	x	x				7				x	x	5	x	x				7				x	x	3
2		x	x	x			5			x	x	x	7	x	x	x			5			x	x	x	7	x	x	x			5			x	x	x	2
1		x	x	5	x	x		x	x	x	x	x	11	x	x	x	x	x		x	x	x	x	x	11	x	x	x	x	x		x	x	5	x	x	1
	36	35	34	33	32	31	30	29	28	27	26	25	24	23	22	21	20	19	18	17	16	15	14	13	12	11	10	9	8	7	6	5	4	3	2	1	

A deciduous forest may consist of many types of different trees, so you might want a bit more variety in your forest blanketscape. This square combines the three leaf types for you so you don't need to read across multiple square patterns. The beech leaf is featured twice because it is the simplest pattern.

One-piece blanket

Repeat each row across the blanket as many times as required for the size you are making. Note: if you have a hard colour change against the previous square, knit across Row 1 for a neater join, instead of working the pattern row.

To join to large or medium leaf patterns:
*Row 1: [P8, k1] four times.
Row 2: [P1, k8] four times.
Row 3: [P8, k1] four times.
Row 4: K5, p2, k2, p1, k2, p2, k11, p5, k6.
Row 5: P5, k7, p8, k5, p1, k1, p1, k5, p3.
Row 6: K2, p15, k6, p9, k4.
Row 7: P3, k11, p5, k15, p2.
Row 8: K3, p13, k6, p11, k3.
Row 9: P2, k13, p6, k11, p4.
Row 10: K3, p13, k5, p13, k2.
Row 11: P2, k13, p4, k15, p2.
Row 12: K2, p15, k4, p13, k2.
Rows 13 and 14: Rep Rows 11 and 12.
Row 15: P2, k13, p4, k15, p2.
Row 16: K2, p3, k1, p7, k1, p3, k4, p13, k2.

Row 17: P2, k13, p4, k2, p2, k7, p2, k2, p2.
Row 18: K2, p1, k3, p7, k3, p1, k5, p11, k3.
Row 19: P3, k11, p9, k7, p6.
Row 20: K7, p5, k11, p9, k4.
Row 21: P4, k9, p11, k5, p7.
Row 22: K7, p5, k12, p7, k5.
Row 23: P6, k5, k14, k3, p8.
Row 24: [P1, k7, p3, k7] twice.
Row 25: [K1, p7] twice, k3, p7, k1, p7, k2.
Row 26: P3, k14, p3, k14, p2.
Row 27: K3, p11, k7, p11, k4.
Row 28: P5, k9, p9, k9, p4.
Row 29: K4, p9, k9, p9, k5.
Row 30: P6, k8, p9, k8, p5.
Row 31: K5, p6, k13, p6, k6.
Row 32: P7, k5, p13, k5, p6.
Row 33: K6, p5, k13, p5, k7.
Row 34: P7, k5, p13, k5, p6.
Row 35: K6, p6, k11, p6, k7.
Row 36: P7, k7, p9, k7, p6.
Row 37: K6, p6, k11, p6, k7.
Row 38: P7, k6, p11, k6, p6.
Rows 39 and 40: Rep Rows 35 and 36.
Row 41: K5, p9, k7, p9, k6.
Row 42: P6, k8, p9, k8, p5.

Row 43: K4, p9, k9, p9, k5.
Row 44: P4, k10, p9, k10, p3.
Row 45: K2, p13, k5, p13, k3.
Row 46: [P1, k8] four times.
Row 47: [P8, k1] four times.
Row 48: [P1, k8] four times******.

To join below small leaf patterns:
Rows 1 to 45: Work as Rows 1 to 45 above.
Row 46: [P1, k17] twice.
Row 47: P5, k1, p23, k1, p5, k1.
Row 48: P1, k5, [p1, k11] twice, p1, k5.

Individual squares

Cast on 36 sts.
Work from * to **.
Cast (bind) off.

To join below small leaf patterns:

	1	2	3	4	5	6	7	8	9	10	11	12	13	14	15	16	17	18	19	20	21	22	23	24	25	26	27	28	29	30	31	32	33	34	35	36	
48		x	x	5	x	x			x	x	x	x	x	11	x	x	x	x	x		x	x	x	x	x	11	x	x	x	x	x		x	x	5	x	x	48
47		x	x	5	x	x			x	x	x	x	x	11	x	x	x	x	x		x	x	x	x	x	23	x	x	x	x	x		x	x	5	x	x	47
46		x	x	x	x	x		x	x	x	x	x	x	17	x	x	x	x	x		x	x	x	x	x	17	x	x	x	x	x		x	x	x	x	x	46

To join to large or medium leaf patterns:

Pattern chart, columns 1–36, rows 1–48 (stitch grid — large mixed leaves).

31 / MEDIUM MIXED LEAVES

This square combines the medium size leaves and the fruit of the three tree types featured in the book. The burrs of the beech tree and the acorns of the oak trees use a similar base pattern so it was straightforward to interchange one for the other in this square.

One-piece blanket

Repeat each row across the blanket as many times as required for the size you are making. Note: if you have a hard colour change against the previous square, knit across Row 1 for a neater join, instead of working the pattern row.

To join to large or medium leaf patterns:
Row 1: [P8, k1] four times.
Row 2: [P1, k8] four times.
Row 3: [P8, k1] four times.
Row 4: K4, p3, k2, p1, k2, p3, k10, p5, k6.
Row 5: P5, k7, p8, k5, p1, k1, p1, k5, p3.
Row 6: K3, p13, k7, p9, k4.
Row 7: P4, k9, p8, k11, p4.
Row 8: K5, p9, k8, p11, k3.
Row 9: P3, k11, p7, k11, p4.
Row 10: K3, p13, k6, p11, k3.
Row 11: P3, k11, p6, k13, p3.
Rows 12 and 13: Rep Rows 10 and 11.
Row 14: K3, p3, k1, p5, k1, p3, k6, p11, k3.
Row 15: P4, k9, p7, k2, p2, k5, p2, k2, p3.
Row 16: K3, p1, k3, p5, k3, p1, k7, p9, k4.
Row 17: P5, k7, p12, k5, p7.
Row 18: K7, p5, k12, p7, k5
Row 19: P3, k1, p2, k5, p2, k1, p11, k3, p8.
Row 20: K8, p3, k10, [p3, k2] three times.

Row 21: [P1, k1] three times, [p2, k1] twice, [p1, k1] twice, p5, k2, p3, k1, p3, k2, p4.
Row 22: K3, p4, k5, p4, k4, p5, k5, p5, k1.
Row 23: P1, k5, p5, k5, p4, k4, p5, k4, p3.
Row 24: [K3, p5] twice, k4, p5, k5, p5, k1.
Row 25: P2, k3, p7, k3, p6, k4, p3, k4, p4.
Row 26: K5, p3, k3, [p3, k7] twice, p3, k2.
Row 27: P3, [k1, p4] twice, k1, p9, [k1, p1] three times, k1, p6.
Row 28: P1, k6, p5, k6, [p1, k3] twice, p3, k3, p1, k3.
Row 29: [K1, p2] twice, k5, p2, k1, p2, k3, p5, k5, p5, k2.
Row 30: P3, k4, p5, k5, p3, k5, p5, k4, p2.
Row 31: K3, p3, k5, p3, k7, p5, k1, p5, k4.
Row 32: P4, k5, p1, k5, p7, k4, p1, k1, p1, k4, p3.
Row 33: K4, p2, [k1, p1] twice, k1, p3, k7, p5, k1, p4, k5.
Row 34: P5, k4, p1, k3, p11, k2, p1, k1, p1, k3, p4.
Row 35: K5, p3, k1, p3, k11, p7, k6.
Row 36: P6, k7, p11, k3, p1, k3, p5.
Row 37: K5, p3, k1, p4, k9, p8, k6.
Row 38: P6, k9, p7, k9, p5.
Row 39: K5, p8, k9, p8, k6.
Row 40: P6, k8, p9, k8, p5.
Row 41: K5, p8, k9, p8, k6.

Row 42: [P5, k11] twice, p4.
Row 43: K4, p10, k7, p10, k5.
Row 44: P4, k11, p7, k11, p3.
Row 45: K2, p12, k7, p12, k3.
Row 46: [P1, k8] four times.
Row 47: [P8, k1] four times.
Row 48: [P1, k8] four times**.

To join below small leaf patterns:
Rows 1 to 45: Work as Rows 1 to 45 above.
Row 46: [P1, k17] twice.
Row 47: P5, k1, p23, k1, p5, k1.
Row 48: P1, k5, [p1, k11] twice, p1, k5.

Individual squares

Cast on 36 sts.

Work from * to **.

Cast (bind) off.

To join below small leaf patterns:

	1	2	3	4	5	6	7	8	9	10	11	12	13	14	15	16	17	18	19	20	21	22	23	24	25	26	27	28	29	30	31	32	33	34	35	36	
48		x	x	5	x	x			x	x	x	x	x	11	x	x	x	x	x		x	x	x	x	x	x	11	x	x	x	x			x	x	5	x	x	48
47		x	x	5	x	x			x	x	x	x	x		x	x	x	x	x		x	x	x	x	x	23	x	x	x	x				x	x	5	x	x	47
46		x	x	x	x	x	x	x	x	x	x	x	17	x	x	x	x	x		x	x	x	x	x	x	17	x	x	x	x	x	x	x	x	x	x	x	46

To join to large or medium leaf patterns:

	1	2	3	4	5	6	7	8	9	10	11	12	13	14	15	16	17	18	19	20	21	22	23	24	25	26	27	28	29	30	31	32	33	34	35	36	
48		x	x	x	x	x	x	8	x		x	8	x	x	x	x	x	x		x	x	x	x	x	x	8	x		x	8	x	x	x	x	x		48
47		x	x	x	x	x	x	8	x		x	8	x	x	x	x	x	x		x	x	x	x	x	x	8	x		x	8	x	x	x	x	x		47
46			x	x	x	x	x	8	x		x	8	x	x	x	x	x	x		x	x	x	x	x	x	8	x		x	8	x	x	x	x	x		46
45			x	x	x	x	x	x	12	x	x	x	x	x				7				x	x	x	x	x	12	x	x	x	x						45
44		4			x	x	x	x	11	x	x	x	x	x				7				x	x	x	x	x	11	x	x	x	x						44
43		5				x	x	x	10	x	x	x	x	x				7				x	x	x	x	x	10	x	x	x				4			43
42		5			x	x	x	x	11	x	x	x	x	x	x			5			x	x	x	x	x	x	11	x	x	x	x			4			42
41		6			x	x	x	8	x	x	x	x				9				x	x	x	x	8	x	x	x						5			41
40		6			x	x	x	8	x	x	x	x				9				x	x	x	x	8	x	x	x						5			40
39		6			x	x	x	8	x	x	x	x				9				x	x	x	x	8	x	x	x						5			39
38		6			x	x	x	9	x	x	x	x	x			7				x	x	x	x	9	x	x	x						5			38
37		6			x	x	x	8	x	x	x	x				9				x	x	4	x										5			37
36		6			x	x	x	7	x	x	x				11					x	x	x			x	x	x						5			36
35		6			x	x	x	7	x	x	x				11					x	x	x			x	x	x						5			35
34		5			x	4	x	x		x	x	x				11				x	x			x			x	x	x				4			34
33		5			x	4	x	x		x	x	x	5	x			7			x	x	x		x			x		x	x			4			33
32		4		x	x	5	x		x	x	x		5	x			7			x	4	x	x		x			x	x	x	4	x				32
31		4		x	x	5	x		x	x	x		5	x			7			x	x	x		5			x	x	x							31
30				x	x	4	x		5			x	5	x	x	x			x	x	5	x	x		5			x	x	4	x					30
29			x	x	x	5	x		5			x	5	x	x	x			x	x		x	x		5			x	x		x	x				29
28		x	x	x	x	6	x		5			x	6	x	x	x	x		x	x		x	x					x	x		x	x	x			28
27	x	x	x	x	6	x	x		x		x		x		x	x	x	x	9	x	x	x		x	4	x		x	4	x	x		x	x	x		27
26	x	x	x	x	5	x			x	x	x			x	x	x	x	7	x	x			x	x	x	7	x	x	x					x	x		26
25	x	4	x	x		4			x	x	x		4		x	x	x	6	x	x			x	x	x	7	x	x	x					x	x		25
24	x	x	x			5			x	x	x			5		x	x	4	x			5			x	x	5	x	x			5			x		24
23	x	x	x			4			x	x	5	x	x		4		x	x	4	x			5			x	x	5	x	x			5			x	23
22	x	x	x			4			x	x	5	x	x		4		x	x	4	x			5			x	x	5	x	x			5			x	22
21	x	x	4	x				x	x	x		x	x	x			x	x	5	x		x			x			x	x		x			x		x	21
20	x	x	x	8	x	x	x	x			x	x		x	x	x	x	x	10	x	x				x	x			x	x				x	x		20
19	x	x	x	8	x	x	x	x			x	x		x	x	x	x	x	11	x	x	x			5			x	x			x	x		x		19
18	x	x	x	7	x	x	x			5			x	x	x	x	x	x	12	x	x	x	x	x			7				x	x	x	x	5	x	18
17	x	x	x	7	x	x	x			5			x	x	x	x	x	x	12	x	x	x	x	x			7				x	x	x	x	5	x	17
16	x	x	x			x	x	x		5			x	x	x	x	x	7	x	x	x	x					9				x	x	x	x	4	x	16
15	x	x	x			x	x		5			x	x			x	x	7	x	x	x	x					9					x	x	x	4	x	15
14	x	x	x				x		5			x			x	x	6	x	x	x					11						x	x	x	x	x		14
13	x	x	x					13						x	x	6	x	x	x					11							x	x	x	x	x		13
12	x	x	x					13						x	x	6	x	x	x					11							x	x	x	x	x		12
11	x	x	x					13						x	x	6	x	x	x					11							x	x	x	x	x		11
10	x	x	x					13						x	x	6	x	x	x					11							x	x	x	x	x		10
9	x	4	x	x				11					x	x	x		x	x	7	x	x				11							x	x	x	x		9
8	x	5	x	x	x			9				x	x	x	x	x	x	8	x	x				11							x	x	x	x	x		8
7	x	4	x	x				11				x	x	x	x	x	8	x	x	x			9								x	x	x	4	x		7
6	x	x	x					13				x	x	x	x	7	x	x	x	x			9								x	x	x	4	x		6
5	x	x	x			5			x		x			5		x	x	8	x	x	x	x			7			x	x	x	x	x	5	x			5
4	x	x	x	x				x	x		x	x			x	x	10	x	x	x	x	x	x			5			x	x	x	x	x	6	x		4
3		x	8	x	x	x	x	x	x		x	x	x	x	x	x	8	x		x	8	x	x	x	x	x		x	x	x	x	x	x	8	x		3
2		x	8	x	x	x	x	x	x		x	x	x	x	x	x	8	x		x	8	x	x	x	x		x	x	x	x	x	x	x	8	x		2
1		x	8	x	x	x	x	x	x		x	x	x	x	x	x	8	x		x	8	x	x	x	x		x	x	x	x	x	x	x	8	x		1

36	35	34	33	32	31	30	29	28	27	26	25	24	23	22	21	20	19	18	17	16	15	14	13	12	11	10	9	8	7	6	5	4	3	2	1

32 / SMALL MIXED LEAVES

One-piece blanket

Repeat each row across the blanket as many times as required for the size you are making. Note: if you have a hard colour change against the previous square, knit across Row 1 for a neater join, instead of working the pattern row.

To join to small leaf patterns:
Row 1: [P5, k1] six times.
Row 2: P1, k3, p5, k3, p1, k2, p2, k1, p1, k1, p2, k2, p1, k4, p3, k4.
Row 3: P3, k5, p3, k1, p1, k9, p1, k1, p2, k7, p2, k1.
Row 4: K3, p7, k4, p9, k5, p5, k3.
Row 5: P2, k7, p4, k9, p5, k5, p4.
Row 6: K3, [p7, k5] twice, p7, k2.
Row 7: P2, k7, p4, k9, p3, k9, p2.
Row 8: K2, p9, k3, p9, k4, p7, k2.
Row 9: P2, k7, p4, k9, p3, k1, p1, k5, p1, k1, p2.
Row 10: K3, p7, k4, p2, k1, p3, k1, p2, k5, p5, k3.
Row 11: P3, k5, p5, k1, p2, k3, p2, k1, p4, k7, p3.
Row 12: [P1, k4, p3, k4] three times.
Row 13: K1, [p3, k3] five times, p3, k2.
Row 14: P2, [k4, p1, k4, p3] twice, k4, p1, k4, p1.
Row 15: K1, p2, k1, p4, k7, p6, k5, p5, k1, p2, k2.

Row 16: P2, k1, p2, k5, p5, k6, p7, k4, p2, k1, p1.
Row 17: K4, p3, k1, p1, k5, p1, k1, p4, k7, p4, k5.
Row 18: P5, k4, p7, k4, p9, k3, p4.
Row 19: K4, p3, k9, p4, k7, p4, k5.
Row 20: P4, [k5, p7] twice, k5, p3.
Row 21: K4, p5, k5, p6, k7, p4, k5.
Row 22: P5, k5, p5, k6, p7, k4, p4
Row 23: K4, p1, k1, p2, k7, p2, k1, p3, k5, p3, k1, p1, k5.
Row 24: P1, k1, p2, k2, p1, k4, p3, k4, p1, k3, p5, k3, p1, k2, p2, k1.
Rows 25 to 48: Rep Rows 1 to 24**.

To join above large or medium leaf patterns:

Row 1: P5, [k1, p11] twice, k1, p5, k1.
Row 2: P1, k3, p5, k6, p2, k1, p1, k1, p2, k7, p3, k4.
Row 3: P3, k5, p5, k9, p4, k7, p2, k1.
Rows 4 to 48: Work as Rows 4 to 48 above (working Rows 1 to 3 as above for Rows 25 to 27).

Individual squares

Cast on 36 sts.

Work from * to **.

Cast (bind) off.

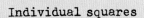

Small Mixed Leaves follows the design of Large Mixed Leaves, but as in similar squares they are smaller in size due to perspective. If you want to join these above Medium or Large Mixed Leaves, you will need the alternative instructions here and for the large or medium leaf you wish to join it to.

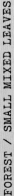

To join to small leaf patterns:

#	1	2	3	4	5	6	7	8	9	10	11	12	13	14	15	16	17	18	19	20	21	22	23	24	25	26	27	28	29	30	31	32	33	34	35	36	#
48		x				x	x		x	x	x	x				x	x	x	x		x	x	x					x	x	x		x	x			x	48
47						x											x	x	x		x								x	x							47
46						x	x	x	x	x							x	x	x		x	x							x	x	x	x	x				46
45							x	x	x	x							x	x	x	x	x	x	x					x		x	x						45
44					x	x	x	x	x								x	x	x	x	x							x	x	x	x	x	x				44
43						x	x	x	x								x	x	x	x									x	x							43
42						x	x	x	x								x	x	x	x									x	x	x						42
41																		x	x	x			x						x		x	x	x				41
40		x				x	x	x	x								x	x	x	x								x	x	x	x				x		40
39			x	x		x	x	x	x								x	x	x	x	x							x	x	x	x		x	x			39
38		x	x	x	x		x	x	x	x	x			x	x	x	x		x	x	x	x			x	x	x	x		x	x	x	x	x			38
37			x	x	x				x	x	x			x	x	x			x	x	x				x	x	x				x	x	x				37
36		x	x	x	x			x	x	x	x	x		x	x	x	x			x	x	x	x		x	x	x	x			x	x	x	x	x		36
35	x	x	x						x	x	x	x		x	x			x	x		x	x		x	x	x	x	x				x	x	x			35
34	x	x	x						x	x	x	x		x			x			x	x		x	x	x	x	x					x	x	x			34
33	x	x		x						x	x	x								x	x	x	x									x	x	x			33
32	x	x								x	x	x								x	x	x	x									x	x	x			32
31	x	x								x	x	x								x	x	x	x									x	x	x			31
30	x	x	x						x	x	x	x	x							x	x	x	x	x								x	x	x			30
29	x	x	x	x				x		x	x	x	x							x	x	x	x									x	x	x			29
28	x	x	x						x	x	x	x	x							x	x	x	x	x	x							x	x	x			28
27		x	x							x	x		x								x			x	x	x						x	x	x			27
26		x	x	x	x					x	x	x		x	x		x			x			x	x			x	x	x	x			x	x	x		26
25		x	x	x	x	x	x		x	x	x	x		x	x		x	x	x	x		x	x		x	x	x	x		x	x	x		x	x		25
24		x			x	x		x	x	4	x			x	4	x	x		x	x	x			5			x	x	x		x	x	x			x	24
23		5				x		x	x	x			5		x	x	x		x	x			7			x	x		x			4					23
22		5				x	5	x	x	x			5		x	x	x	6	x	x			7			x	x	4	x			4					22
21		5			x	x	4	x	x				7			x	x	6	x	x	x		5		x	x	x	x	5	x		4					21
20		4		x	x	x	5	x	x				7			x	x	5	x	x			7		x	x	x	5	x	x							20
19		5			x	4	x	x					7			x	x	4	x				9				x	x	x			4					19
18		5			x	4	x	x					7			x	x	4	x				9				x	x	x			4					18
17		5			x	4	x						7			x	x	4	x		x		5			x			x			4					17
16		x			x	5	x	x	x				5		x	x	x	6	x	x			7			x	x	4	x			x					16
15			x	x		x	5	x	x	x			5		x	x	x	6	x	x			7			x	x	4	x		x	x					15
14		x	4	x	x		x	x	4	x			x	4	x	x		x	x	4	x			x	4	x	x		x	4	x	x	x				14
13		x	x	x				x	x	x			x	x	x		x	x	x			x	x	x			x	x	x		x	x					13
12		x	4	x			x	4	x	x		x	x	4	x	x	4	x	x		x	4	x	x		x	x	4	x		x	4	x	x			12
11	x	x	x				7			x	4	x	x	x	x		x	x			x	x	x	x	5	x	x		5			x	x				11
10	x	x	x				7			x	4	x	x		x		x	x		x	5	x	x		x	5	x	x		5			x	x			10
9	x	x		x			5			x		x	x	x				9			x	4	x	x			7					x	x				9
8	x	x					9			x	x	x					9			x	4	x	x			7					x	x				8
7	x	x					9			x	x	x					9			x	4	x	x			7					x	x				7
6	x	x	x				7		x	x	5	x	x			7			x	x	5	x	x			7					x	x	x			6
5	x	4	x	x			5		x	x	x	x				9			x	4	x	x			7					x	x				5
4	x	x	x				7		x	x	4	x				9			x	5	x	x			5			x	x	x					4
3		x	x				7		x	x	x				9			x			x			5			x	x	x			3				3
2		x	x	x			5		x	x	x		x		x		x			x			x	4	x	x			x	x	4	x				2
1		x	x	5	x	x		x	x	5	x	x		x	x	5	x	x		x	x	5	x	x		x	x	5	x	x		x	x	5	x	x	1

| 36 | 35 | 34 | 33 | 32 | 31 | 30 | 29 | 28 | 27 | 26 | 25 | 24 | 23 | 22 | 21 | 20 | 19 | 18 | 17 | 16 | 15 | 14 | 13 | 12 | 11 | 10 | 9 | 8 | 7 | 6 | 5 | 4 | 3 | 2 | 1 |

To join above large or medium leaf patterns:

#																																					#
3		x	x				7			x	x	4	x					9							x	5	x	x	x			5			x	x	x	3
2		x	x	x			5		x	x	x	6	x	x			x		x			x	x	7	x	x	x	x			x	x	4	x		2
1		x	x	5	x	x		x	x	x	x	x	11	x	x	x	x	x		x	x	x	x	11	x	x	x	x		x	x	5	x	x	1

| 36 | 35 | 34 | 33 | 32 | 31 | 30 | 29 | 28 | 27 | 26 | 25 | 24 | 23 | 22 | 21 | 20 | 19 | 18 | 17 | 16 | 15 | 14 | 13 | 12 | 11 | 10 | 9 | 8 | 7 | 6 | 5 | 4 | 3 | 2 | 1 |

Mountain

Mountain landscapes are big landscapes, so the scale of the features changes for this section compared to previous ones. We are taking a distant perspective of trees and foothills, with majestic mountains looming in the background.

Where we considered individual leaves in the forest section, we are now concerned with groups of coniferous trees distant in the landscape. The patterns start with **Large Conifer Trees** in the foreground, equally spaced to enable their features to show. These are based on the 'happy little trees' of the artist Bob Ross, likely a white spruce from the Alaskan landscapes that he painted. His TV shows in the 80s and 90s split opinion, but the trees he painted had a simple and repeatable form – which is exactly what is required for the repeating patterns in this book. **Small Conifer Trees** places the trees further into the distance, with perspective leading them to appear smaller. Combined Conifers shows how these patterns can be combined for a smaller blanket, such as the **Snowy Mountains** blanket.

Beyond the small conifers are a group of misty foothills represented in **Foothills**. These are smaller, more rounded hills, before we reach the larger craggy mountains. Often the mist might sit in the valleys between the hills, accentuating the pattern the hills make. Looming high above the mist are the craggy mountains – bright on the side facing the sun and casting shade in their lee. The mountains repeat into the distance in **Mountains**. The foothills and mountains are featured together in **Combined Mountains**.

One-piece blanket

Repeat each row across the blanket as many times as required for the size you are making.

*Row 1: K to end.
Row 2: P8, k1, p1, k1, p15, k1, p1, k1, p7.
Row 3: K7, p1, k1, p1, k15, p1, k1, p1, k8.
Row 4: P8, k8, p10, k8, p2.
Row 5: K3, p12, k6, p12, k3.
Row 6: P4, k9, p9, k9, p5.
Row 7: K6, p6, k12, p6, k6.
Row 8: P7, k8, p10, k8, p3.
Row 9: K4, p10, k8, p10, k4.
Row 10: P5, k7, p11, k7, p6.
Row 11: K7, p4, k14, p4, k7.
Row 12: P8, k6, p12, k6, p4.
Row 13: K5, p8, k10, p8, k5.
Row 14: P6, k5, p13, k5, p7.
Row 15: K8, p2, k16, p2, k8.
Row 16: P9, k4, p14, k4, p5.
Row 17: K6, p6, k12, p6, k6.
Row 18: P7, k4, p14, k4, p7.
Row 19: K8, p2, k16, p2, k8.
Row 20: P9, k3, p15, k3, p6.
Row 21: K7, p4, k14, p4, k7.
Row 22: P8, k2, k16, p2, p8.
Row 23: K8, p1, k17, p1, k9.
Row 24: P9, k1, p17, k1, p8.
Row 25: K to end.
Row 26: [P1, k1, p15, k1] twice.
Row 27: [P1, k15, p1, k1] twice.
Row 28: K7, p10, k8, p10, k1.
Row 29: P6, k6, p12, k6, p6.
Row 30: K4, p9, k9, p9, k5.
Row 31: P3, k12, p6, k12, p3.
Row 32: K6, p10, k8, p10, k2.
Row 33: P5, k8, p10, k8, p5.
Row 34: K3, p11, k7, p11, k4.
Row 35: P2, k14, p4, k14, p2.
Row 36: K5, p12, k6, p12, k1.
Row 37: P4, k10, p8, k10, p4.
Row 38: K2, p13, k5, p13, k3.
Row 39: P1, k16, p2, k16, p1.
Row 40: [K4, p14] twice.
Row 41: P3, k12, p6, k12, p3.
Row 42: K2, p14, k4, p14, k2.
Row 43: P1, k16, p2, k16, p1.
Row 44: [K3, p15] twice.
Row 45: P2, k14, p4, k14, p2.
Row 46: K1, p16, k2, p16, k1.
Row 47: [K17, p1] twice.
Row 48: [K1, p17] twice**.

Individual squares

Cast on 36 sts.

Work from * to **.

Row 49: K to end.

Cast (bind) off purlwise.

One-piece blanket

Repeat each row across the blanket as many times as required for the size you are making.

*Row 1: K to end.
Row 2: P3, [k1, p1, k1, p6] three times, k1, p1, k1, p3.
Row 3: K3, [p1, k1, p1, k6] three times, p1, k1, p1, k3.
Row 4: P1, [k7, p2] three times, k7, p1.
Row 5: K2, [p5, k4] three times, p5, k2.
Row 6: P3, [k3, p6] three times, k3, p3.
Rows 7 and 8: Rep Rows 5 and 6.
Row 9: K4, [p1, k8] three times, p1, k4.
Row 10: P3, [k3, p6] three times, k3, p3.
Row 11: K4, [p1, k8] three times, p1, k4.
Row 12: P4, [k1, p8] three times, k1, p4.
Row 13: K to end.
Row 14: [P1, k1, p6, k1] four times.
Row 15: [P1, k6, p1, k1] four times.
Row 16: K4, [p2, k7] three times, p2, k3.
Row 17: P2, [k4, p5] three times, k4, p3.
Row 18: K2, [p6, k3] three times, p6, k1.
Rows 19 and 20: Rep Rows 17 and 18.
Row 21: [K8, p1] four times.
Row 22: K2, [p6, k3] three times, p6, k1.
Row 23: [K8, p1] four times.
Row 24: [K1, p8] four times.
Rows 25 to 48: Rep Rows 1 to 24**.

Individual squares

Cast on 36 sts.

Work from * to **.

Row 49: K to end.

Cast (bind) off purlwise.

Conifers are commonly found in plantations, so the layout of the trees can be quite regular. The spacing between the trees varies, sometimes growing close together and competing for light, or well spaced out. To keep the square pattern simple to follow, the conifer trees here are well spaced and in a regular formation.

One-piece blanket

Repeat each row across the blanket as many times as required for the size you are making.

*Row 1: K to end.
Row 2: P8, k1, p1, k1, p15, k1, p1, k1, p7.
Row 3: K7, p1, k1, p1, k15, p1, k1, p1, k8.
Row 4: P8, k8, p10, k8, p2.
Row 5: K3, p12, k6, p12, k3.
Row 6: P4, k9, p9, k9, p5.
Row 7: K6, p6, k12, p6, k6.
Row 8: P7, k8, p10, k8, p3.
Row 9: K4, p10, k8, p10, k4.
Row 10: P5, k7, p11, k7, p6.
Row 11: K7, p4, k14, p4, k7.
Row 12: P8, k6, p12, k6, p4.
Row 13: K5, p8, k10, p8, k5.
Row 14: P6, k5, p13, k5, p7.
Row 15: K8, p2, k16, p2, k8.
Row 16: P9, k4, p14, k4, p5.
Row 17: K6, p6, k12, p6, k6.
Row 18: P7, k4, p14, k4, p7.
Row 19: K8, p2, k16, p2, k8.
Row 20: P9, k3, p15, k3, p6.
Row 21: K7, p4, k14, p4, k7.
Row 22: P8, k2, p16, k2, p8.
Row 23: K8, p1, k17, p1, k9.
Row 24: P9, k1, p17, k1, p8.
Row 25: K to end.
Row 26: P3, [k1, p1, k1, p6] three times, k1, p1, k1, p3.
Row 27: K3, [p1, k1, p1, k6] three times, p1, k1, p1, k3.
Row 28: P1, [k7, p2] three times, k7, p1.
Row 29: K2, [p5, k4] three times, p5, k2.

Row 30: P3, [k3, p6] three times, k3, p3.
Rows 31 and 32: Rep Rows 29 and 30.
Row 33: K4, [p1, k8] three times, p1, k4.
Row 34: P3, [k3, p6] three times, k3, p3.
Row 35: K4, [p1, k8] three times, p1, k4.
Row 36: P4, [k1, p8] three times, k1, p4.
Row 37: K to end.
Row 38: [P1, k1, p6, k1] four times.
Row 39: [P1, k6, p1, k1] four times.
Row 40: K4, [p2, k7] three times, p2, k3.
Row 41: P2, [k4, p5] three times, k4, p3.
Row 42: K2, [p6, k3] three times, p6, k1.
Rows 43 and 44: Rep Rows 41 and 42.
Row 45: [K8, p1] four times.
Row 46: K2, [p6, k3] three times, p6, k1.
Row 47: [K8, p1] four times.
Row 48: [K1, p8] four times**.

Individual squares

Cast on 36 sts.

Work from * to **.

Row 49: K to end.
Cast (bind) off purlwise.

For a smaller baby blanket you might want to combine the two conifer patterns into a smaller square. This square provides you with a ready-made combination of the two previous patterns.

One-piece blanket

Repeat each row across the blanket as many times as required for the size you are making.

*Row 1: K to end.
Row 2: P5, k8, p10, k8, p5.
Row 3: K2, p14, k4, p14, k2.
Row 4: [P1, k17] twice.
Row 5: [K1, p17] twice.
Row 6: P2, k14, p4, k14, p2.
Row 7: K3, p12, k6, p12, k3.
Row 8: P4, k10, p8, k10, p4.
Row 9: K5, p8, k10, p8, k5.
Row 10: P6, k6, p12, k6, p6.
Row 11: K7, p4, k14, p4, k7.
Row 12: P8, k2, p16, k2, p8.
Row 13: K to end.
Row 14: K4, p10, k2, p1, k5, p10, k2, p1, k1.
Row 15: P2, k1, p4, k4, p9, k1, p4, k4, p7.
Row 16: K14, p1, k17, p1, k3.
Row 17: P4, k1, p17, k1, k13.
Row 18: K12, p4, k14, p4, k2.
Row 19: P1, k6, p12, k6, p11.
Row 20: [K10, p8] twice.
Row 21: K9, p8, k10, p8, k1.
Row 22: P2, k6, p12, k6, p10.
Row 23: K11, p4, k14, p4, k3.
Row 24: P4, k2, p16, k2, p12.
Row 25: K to end.
Row 26: [P10, k8] twice.
Row 27: P11, k4, p14, k4, p3.
Row 28: K5, p1, k17, p1, k12.
Row 29: P13, k1, p17, k1, p4.
Row 30: K3, p4, k14, p4, k11.

Row 31: P10, k6, p12, k6, p2.
Row 32: K1, p8, k10, p8, k9.
Row 33: [P8, k10] twice.
Row 34: P11, k6, p12, k6, p1.
Row 35: K2, p4, k14, p4, k12.
Row 36: P13, k2, p16, k2, p3.
Row 37: K to end.
Row 38: P1, k8, p10, k8, p9.
Row 39: P2, k4, p1, k1, p12, k4, p1, k1, p10.
Row 40: K9, p1, k17, p1, k8.
Row 41: P9, k1, p17, k1, p8.
Row 42: K7, p4, k14, p4, k7.
Row 43: P6, k6, p12, k6, p6.
Row 44: K5, p8, k10, p8, k5.
Row 45: P4, k10, p8, k10, p4.
Row 46: K3, p12, k6, p12, k3.
Row 47: P2, k14, p4, k14, p2.
Row 48: K1, p16, k2, p16, k1 ******.

Individual squares

Cast on 36 sts.

Work from * to **.

Row 49: K to end.
Cast (bind) off purlwise.

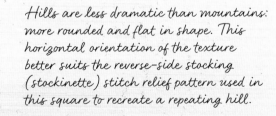

Hills are less dramatic than mountains: more rounded and flat in shape. This horizontal orientation of the texture better suits the reverse-side stocking (stockinette) stitch relief pattern used in this square to recreate a repeating hill.

Chart — columns 1–36 (top), rows 1–48 (left & right), columns 36–1 (bottom)

Top column headers: 1 2 3 4 5 6 7 8 9 10 11 12 13 14 15 16 17 18 19 20 21 22 23 24 25 26 27 28 29 30 31 32 33 34 35 36

Row	Pattern (left → right)
48	x … 16 … x x … 16 … x
47	x x … 14 … x 4 x x … 14 … x x
46	x x x … 12 … x x 6 x x x … 12 … x x x
45	x 4 x x … 10 … x x x 8 x x x x … 10 … x x 4 x
44	x 5 x x x … 8 … x x x x 10 x x x x x … 8 … x x x x 5 x
43	x 6 x x x x … 6 … x x x x x 12 x x x x x x … 6 … x x x x x 6 x
42	x 7 x x x x x … 4 … x x x x x x 14 x x x x x x x … 4 … x x x x x x 7 x
41	x 8 x x x x x x … x x x x x x x 17 x x x x x x x x … x x x x x x x x 9 x
40	x 9 x x x x x x x … x x x x x x 17 x x x x x x x x x … x x x x x x x x 8 x
39	x 10 x x x x x x x x … x 4 … x x x x x x 12 x x x x … x … 4 … x x x
38	x x x 8 x x x x … 10 … x x x x 8 x x x x … 9
37	
36	13 … x x … 16 … x x
35	12 … x 4 x x … 14 … x 4 x x
34	11 … x x 6 x x x … 12 … x x 6 x x x
33	10 … x x x 8 x x x x … 10 … x x x 8 x x x x
32	x … 8 … x x x x 10 x x x x x … 8 … x x x x 9 x x x x
31	x x … 6 … x x x x x 12 x x x x x … 6 … x x x x x 10 x x x x
30	x x x … 4 … x x x x x x 14 x x x x x x … 4 … x x x x x x 11 x x x x
29	x 4 x x … x x x x x x x 17 x x x x x x x … x x x x x x x 13 x x x x
28	x 5 x x x … x x x x x x x 17 x x x x x x x x … x x x x x x x 12 x x x x
27	x x x … 4 … x x x x x x x 14 x x x x x x x … 4 … x x x x x x x 11 x x x x
26	10 … x x x 8 x x x x … 10 … x x x 8 x x x x
25	
24	4 … x x … 16 … x x … 12
23	x 4 x x … 14 … x 4 x x … 11
22	x x 6 x x x … 12 … x x 6 x x x … 10
21	x x x 8 x x x x … 10 … x x x 8 x x x x … 9
20	x x x x 10 x x x x x … 8 … x x x 10 x x x x x … 8
19	x x x x 11 x x x x x x … 6 … x x x x 12 x x x x x x … x
18	x x x x 12 x x x x x x x … 4 … x x x x 14 x x x x x x x … 4 … x x
17	x x x x 13 x x x x x x x x … x x x x 17 x x x x x x x … x x 4 x
16	x x x x 14 x x x x x x x x x … x x x x 17 x x x x x x x x … x x x
15	x 7 x x x x x … 4 … x 4 x x … x x 9 x x x x x … 4 … x 4 x x … x x
14	x 4 x x … 10 … x x … x 5 x x x … 10 … x x
13	
12	8 … x x … 16 … x x … 8
11	7 … x 4 x x … 14 … x 4 x x … 7
10	6 … x x 6 x x x … 12 … x x 6 x x x … 6
9	5 … x x x 8 x x x x … 10 … x x x 8 x x x x … 5
8	4 … x x x x 10 x x x x x … 8 … x x x x 10 x x x x x … 4
7	x x x x x 12 x x x x x x … 6 … x x x x 12 x x x x x x
6	x x x x x 14 x x x x x x x … 4 … x x x x 14 x x x x x x x
5	x x x x x x 17 x x x x x x x … x x x x 17 x x x x x x x x
4	x x x x x x 17 x x x x x x x … x x x x 17 x x x x x x x x x
3	x x x x x 14 x x x x x x … 4 … x x x x 14 x x x x x x
2	5 … x x x 8 x x x x … 10 … x x x 8 x x x x … 5
1	

Bottom column headers: 36 35 34 33 32 31 30 29 28 27 26 25 24 23 22 21 20 19 18 17 16 15 14 13 12 11 10 9 8 7 6 5 4 3 2 1

One-piece blanket

Repeat each row across the blanket as many times as required for the size you are making.

*Row 1: K to end.
Row 2: P4, k5, p13, k5, p1, k5, p3.
Row 3: K1, p6, k3, p6, k12, p6, k2.
Row 4: K7, p11, k7, p5, k6.
Row 5: P5, k7, p7, k11, p6.
Row 6: K5, p11, k7, p9, k4.
Row 7: P3, k10, p7, k11, p5.
Row 8: K4, p11, k7, p11, k3.
Row 9: P2, k1, p1, k10, p6, k1, p1, k10, p4.
Row 10: K4, p10, k1, p1, k6, p10, k1, p1, k2.
Row 11: P1, k3, p1, k10, p4, k3, p1, k10, p3.
Row 12: K3, p9, k1, p4, k4, p9, k1, p4, k1.
Row 13: [K5, p1, k9, p3] twice.
Row 14: [K3, p8, k1, p6] twice.
Row 15: P1, k5, p2, k7, p4, k5, p2, k7, p3.
Row 16: [P1, k3, p6, k3, p4, k1] twice.
Row 17: K1, p1, k3, p4, k5, p3, k2, p1, k3, p4, k5, p3, k1.
Row 18: P2, k2, p5, k1, p1, k3, p2, k1, p3, k2, p5, k1, p1, k3, p2, k1, p1.
Row 19: K2, p1, k1, p2, k3, p1, k4, p2, k4, p1, k1, p2, k3, p1, k4, p2, k2.
Row 20: P3, k2, p3, k1, p4, k1, p1, k1, p5, k2, p3, k1, p4, k1, p1, k1, p2.
Row 21: K3, p1, k6, p1, k2, p2, [k6, p1] twice, k2, p2, k3.
Row 22: P4, k1, p2, k1, p14, k1, p2, k1, p10.
Row 23: K11, p1, k1, p1, k15, p1, k1, p1, k4.
Row 24: P5, k1, p17, k1, p12.
Row 25: K to end.
Row 26: P9, k5, p1, k5, p7, k5, p4.
Row 27: K5, [p6, k3] twice, p6, k7.
Row 28: P5, k7, p5, k13, p6.
Row 29: K7, p11, k7, p7, k4.
Row 30: P3, k7, p9, k9, p8.
Row 31: K8, p8, k10, p7, k3.
Row 32: P2, k7, p11, k7, p9.
Row 33: K9, p6, k1, p1, k10, p6, k1, p1, k1.
Row 34: P1, k1, p1, k6, p10, k1, p1, k6, p9.
Row 35: [K10, p4, k3, p1] twice.
Row 36: [P4, k4, p9, k1] twice.
Row 37: [P1, k9, p3, k5] twice.
Row 38: P5, k3, p8, k1, p6, k3, p8, k1, p1.
Row 39: K1, p2, k7, p4, k5, p2, k7, p4, k4.
Row 40: [P4, k1, p1, k3, p6, k3] twice.
Row 41: [P4, k5, p3, k2, p1, k3] twice.
Row 42: K1, p2, k1, p3, k2, p5, k1, p1, k3, p2, k1, p3, k2, p5, k1, p1, k2.
Row 43: P1, k3, p1, k4, p2, k4, p1, k1, p2, k3, p1, k4, p2, k4, p1, k1, p1.
Row 44: [K1, p1, k1, p5, k2, p3, k1, p4] twice.
Row 45: K5, p1, k2, p2, [k6, p1] twice, k2, p2, k6, p1, k1.
Row 46: P9, k1, p2, k1, p14, k1, p2, k1, p5.
Row 47: K6, p1, k1, p1, k15, p1, k1, p1, k9.
Row 48: P10, k1, p17, k1, p7**.

Individual squares

Cast on 36 sts.

Work from * to **.

Row 49: K to end.
Cast (bind) off purlwise.

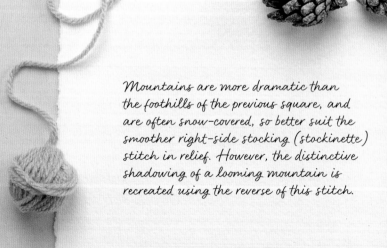

Mountains are more dramatic than the foothills of the previous square, and are often snow-covered, so better suit the smoother right-side stocking (stockinette) stitch in relief. However, the distinctive shadowing of a looming mountain is recreated using the reverse of this stitch.

Knitting chart — columns numbered 1–36 (top) and 36–1 (bottom); rows numbered 48–1 on both sides.

Row	1	2	3	4	5	6	7	8	9	10	11	12	13	14	15	16	17	18	19	20	21	22	23	24	25	26	27	28	29	30	31	32	33	34	35	36	Row
48						10					x									17									x					7			48
47						9					x		x							15								x		x				6			47
46						9					x		x							14								x			x			5			46
45		x				6			x	x			x			6				x				6			x	x			x			5			45
44	x		x			5			x	x				x		4		x		x				5			x	x				x		4			44
43	x		x			4			x	x		4		x			x	x		x				4			x	x			x					x	43
42	x			x					x	x		5			x		x	x	x		x				x	x				5		x			x	x	42
41				x				x	x			5			x	x	x							x	x	x				x		x	x	4	x		41
40		4				x		x	x	x		6				x	x	x			4		x		x	x	x			6			x	x			40
39		4			x	x	4	x				7				x	x			5			x	x	4	x				7			x	x			39
38		5				x	x	x				8					x			6				x	x	x				8				x			38
37		5				x	x	x				9						x		5				x	x	x				9						x	37
36		4				x	x	4	x			9						x		4			x	x	4	x				9						x	36
35	x						x	x	4	x		10							x					x	x	4	x			10							35
34		x			x	x	6	x	x						10					x			x	x	6	x	x							9			34
33		x			x	x	6	x	x						10					x			x	x	6	x	x							9			33
32			x	x	x	x	7	x	x						11							x	x	x	7	x	x							9			32
31			x	x	x		7	x	x	x					10							x	x	x	8	x	x	x						8			31
30			x	x	x		7	x	x	x					9						x	x	x	x	9	x	x	x						8			30
29		4			x		7	x	x	x	x				7				x	x	x	x	x	11	x	x	x	x	x					7			29
28		5				x	x	7	x	x	x				5			x	x	x	x	x	x	13	x	x	x	x	x	x				6			28
27		7						x	x	x	6	x	x				x	x	6	x	x	x			x	x	6	x	x					5			27
26		9								x	x	5	x	x		x	x	5	x	x				7				x	x	5	x	x		4			26
25																																					25
24		5					x								17									x				12									24
23		4			x		x								15							x		x				11									23
22		4			x			x							14							x			x			10									22
21				x	x			x			6				x				6			x	x			x		6			x						21
20				x	x				x		4				x				5			x	x		x			4		x		x					20
19			x				4		x				x	x	x				4			x		4					x	x		x					19
18			x	x			5				x		x	x	x		x					x	x	5			x		x	x	x			x			18
17		x	x	x			5				x	x	4	x			x				x	x		5			x	x	4	x				x			17
16		x	x	x			6				x	x	x			4		x			x	x		6			x	x	x			4			x		16
15	x	x	x				7				x	x				5		x	x	4	x			7			x	x				5			x		15
14	x	x	x				8				x					6			x	x	x			8			x					6			x		14
13	x	x	x				9						x			5			x	x	x			9					x			5			x		13
12	x	x	x				9						x			4		x	x	x	x			9					x			4			x		12
11	x	x	x				10							x				x	x	4	x			10						x					x		11
10	x	4	x	x							10				x		x	x	x	6	x	x			10					x				x	x	x	10
9	x	4	x	x							10				x		x	x	x	6	x	x			10					x				x	x	x	9
8	x	4	x	x							11					x	x	x	x	7	x	x			11								x	x	x	x	8
7	x	5	x	x	x						11					x	x	x	7	x	x	x			10								x	x	x	x	7
6	x	5	x	x	x						11					x	x	x	7	x	x	x			9						x	x	x	4	x	x	6
5	x	6	x	x	x	x					11					x	x	7	x	x					7						x	x	5	x	x	x	5
4	x	7	x	x	x	x	x				11							x	x	x	7	x	x	x				x	x	6	x	x					4
3		x	x	x	6	x	x				12									x	x	x	6	x	x				x	x	6	x	x				3
2		4			x	x	5	x	x		13											x	x	5	x	x			x	x	5	x	x				2
1																																					1

38 / COMBINED MOUNTAINS

One-piece blanket

Repeat each row across the blanket as many times as required for the size you are making.

*Row 1: K to end.
Row 2: P5, k8, p10, k8, p5.
Row 3: K2, p14, k4, p14, k2.
Row 4: [P1, k17] twice.
Row 5: [K1, p17] twice.
Row 6: P2, k14, p4, k14, p2.
Row 7: K3, p12, k6, p12, k3.
Row 8: P4, k10, p8, k10, p4.
Row 9: K5, p8, k10, p8, k5.
Row 10: P6, k6, p12, k6, p6.
Row 11: K7, p4, k14, p4, k7.
Row 12: P8, k2, p16, k2, p8.
Row 13: K to end.
Row 14: K4, p10, k8, p10, k4.
Row 15: P7, k4, p14, k4, p7.
Row 16: K9, p1, k17, p1, k8.
Row 17: P9, k1, p17, k1, p8.
Row 18: K7, p4, k14, p4, k7.
Row 19: P6, k6, p12, k6, p6.
Row 20: K5, p8, k10, p8, k5.
Row 21: P4, k10, p8, k10, p4.
Row 22: K3, p12, k6, p12, k3.
Row 23: P2, k14, p4, k14, p2.
Row 24: K1, p16, k2, p16, k1.
Row 25: K to end.
Row 26: P4, k5, p13, k5, p1, k5, p3.
Row 27: K1, p6, k3, p6, k12, p6, k2.
Row 28: K7, p11, k7, p5, k6.
Row 29: P5, k7, p7, k11, p6.
Row 30: K5, p11, k7, p9, k4.
Row 31: P3, k10, p7, k11, p5.
Row 32: K4, p11, k7, p11, k3.
Row 33: P2, k1, p1, k10, p6, k1, p1, k10, p4.
Row 34: K4, p10, k1, p1, k6, p10, k1, p1, k2.
Row 35: P1, k3, p1, k10, p4, k3, p1, k10, p3.
Row 36: K3, p9, k1, p4, k4, p9, k1, p4, k1.

Row 37: [K5, p1, k9, p3] twice.
Row 38: [K3, p8, k1, p6] twice.
Row 39: P1, k5, p2, k7, p4, k5, p2, k7, p3.
Row 40: [P1, k3, p6, k3, p4, k1] twice.
Row 41: K1, p1, k3, p4, k5, p3, k2, p1, k3, p4, k5, p3, k1.
Row 42: P2, k2, p5, k1, p1, k3, p2, k1, p3, k2, p5, k1, p1, k3, p2, k1, p1.
Row 43: K2, p1, k1, p2, k3, p1, k4, p2, k4, p1, k1, p2, k3, p1, k4, p2, k2.
Row 44: P3, k2, p3, k1, p4, k1, p1, k1, p5, k2, p3, k1, p4, k1, p1, k1, p2.
Row 45: K3, p1, k6, p1, k2, p2, [k6, p1] twice, k2, p2, k3.
Row 46: P4, k1, p2, k1, p14, k1, p2, k1, p10.
Row 47: K11, p1, k1, p1, k15, p1, k1, p1, k4.
Row 48: P5, k1, p17, k1, p12**.

Individual squares

Cast on 36 sts.

Work from * to **.

Row 49: K to end.
Cast (bind) off purlwise.

For a smaller baby blanket you might want to combine the two mountain patterns into a smaller square. In that case, this square provides you with a combination of the two previous patterns.

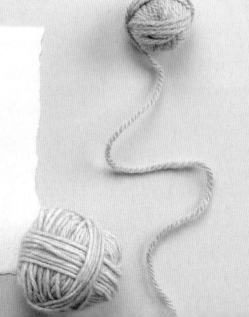

Weather

As we reach the top of the blanket, we look upwards at the sky. Unless you live in sunny warm climes, the sky is an ever-changing part of the landscape. Clouds form shapes that let your imagination run wild as to what they might resemble. Some of the clouds might be rain bearing; in **Rain** it is 'raining stair-rods' – heavy rain that looks like the narrow rods that hold carpet in place on stairs.

The naming conventions for clouds are based on a book "Essay on the Modifications of Clouds" written by Luke Howard in 1803. Clouds are separated into groups based on the elevation at which they occur, and the names are a combination of prefixes and suffixes. The clouds that produce the rain shown in Rain are 'nimbo' or 'nimbus' meaning 'rainy cloud' in Latin. **Lower Stormy Clouds** and **Upper Stormy Clouds** are nimbostratus clouds, the suffix 'stratus' implying a layer, rather than the more dramatic cumulonimbus thunderstorm clouds. Nimbostratus clouds mean the rain is probably set in for a while! **Combined Stormy Clouds** brings together the two patterns for a smaller blanket.

On a fair-weather day, clouds might take the classic 'cumulus' shape; cumulo meaning 'heap' in Latin. These clouds are flat on the bottom and puff up as the air continues to rise. **Small Sunny Clouds** and **Large Sunny Clouds** represent two sizes of fair-weather cumulus clouds, with the clouds at the top of the blanket seeming bigger as they are overhead and, therefore, closer. **Combined Sunny Clouds** unites two sizes of cloud in one square.

Small Winter Clouds, **Medium Winter Clouds** and **Large Winter Clouds** have a simple modification to turn flat-bottomed cumulus clouds into 'altocumulus' clouds; alto meaning 'height' in Latin. These clouds are formed higher than standard cumulus, often caused by instabilities in the atmosphere. Altocumulus clouds can form at any time of year, but I've named them winter clouds to distinguish them from the classic summer cumulus clouds above. **Combined Winter Clouds** combines the small and medium altostratus into a single square.

Looming Clouds represents a looming weather front on the horizon. You might be enjoying a sunny day on the beach, but if these are approaching you'd better finish up your picnic, fold up your blanketscape and head for home!

One-piece blanket

Repeat each row across the blanket as many times as required for the size you are making. Note: if you have a hard colour change against the previous square, knit across Row 1 for a neater join, instead of working the pattern row.

*Row 1: [K1, p1] 18 times.
Row 2: [K1, p1] 18 times.
Row 3: [K1, p3] nine times.
Row 4: [K3, p1] nine times.
Row 5: [K1, p1] 18 times.
Row 6: [K1, p1] 18 times.
Row 7: P2, [k1, p3] eight times, k1, p1.

Row 8: K1, [p1, k3] eight times, p1, k2.
Rows 9 to 48: Rep Rows 1 to 8 five times more**.

Individual squares

Cast on 36 sts.

Work from * to **.

Cast (bind) off.

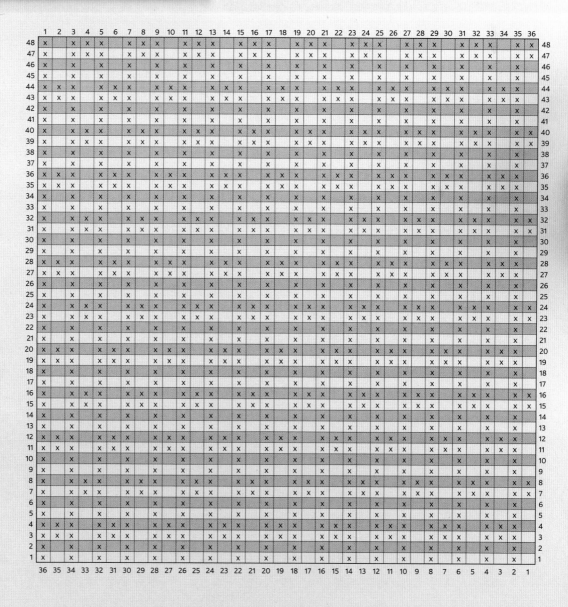

On a dull or rainy day the sky might be covered completely in a blanket of cloud, but there may still be some texture visible in the base of the clouds. Just above the horizon the clouds bases seem narrower due to perspective, which is recreated here using reverse-side stocking (stockinette) stitch.

One-piece blanket

Repeat each row across the blanket as many times as required for the size you are making.

*Rows 1 and 2: St st two rows.
Row 3: K4, p28, k4.
Row 4: P3, k30, p3.
Row 5: K2, p32, k2.
Row 6: P2, k32, p2.
Row 7: K3, p30, k3.
Row 8: P5, k5, p2, k12, p2, k5, p5.
Row 9: K13, p10, k13.
Row 10: P15, k6, p15.
Rows 11 to 14: St st four rows.
Row 15: P23, k8, p5.
Row 16: K6, p6, k24.
Row 17: P25, k4, p7.
Row 18: K7, p4, k25.
Row 19: P24, k6, p6.
Row 20: K4, p10, k5, p2, k12, p2, k1.
Row 21: K4, p10, k22.
Row 22: P24, k6, p6.
Rows 23 to 26: St st four rows.
Row 27: P5, k8, p23.
Row 28: K24, p6, k6.
Row 29: P7, k4, p25.
Row 30: K25, p4, k7.
Row 31: P6, k6, p24.
Row 32: K1, p2, k12, p2, k5, p10, k4.
Row 33: K22, p10, k4.

Row 34: P6, k6, p24.
Rows 35 to 38: St st four rows.
Row 39: P14, k8, p14.
Row 40: K15, p6, k15.
Row 41: P16, k4, p16.
Row 42: K16, p4, k16.
Row 43: P15, k6, p15.
Row 44: K6, p2, k5, p10, k5, p2, k6.
Row 45: P5, k26, p5.
Row 46: K3, p30, k3.
Rows 47 and 48: St st two rows**.

Individual squares

Cast on 36 sts.

Work from * to **.

Cast (bind) off.

	1	2	3	4	5	6	7	8	9	10	11	12	13	14	15	16	17	18	19	20	21	22	23	24	25	26	27	28	29	30	31	32	33	34	35	36	
48																																					48
47																																					47
46	x	x	x															30																x	x	x	46
45	x	5	x	x	x													26															x	x	5	x	45
44	x	6	x	x	x	x			x	x	5	x	x					10						x	x	5	x	x				x	x	x	6	x	44
43	x	15	x	x	x	x	x	x	x	x	x	x	x	x	x			6					x	x	x	x	x	x	x	x	x	x	x	x	15	x	43
42	x	16	x	x	x	x	x	x	x	x	x	x	x	x	x	x		4			x	x	x	x	x	x	x	x	x	x	x	x	x	x	16	x	42
41	x	16	x	x	x	x	x	x	x	x	x	x	x	x	x	x		4			x	x	x	x	x	x	x	x	x	x	x	x	x	x	16	x	41
40	x	15	x	x	x	x	x	x	x	x	x	x	x	x	x			6				x	x	x	x	x	x	x	x	x	x	x	x	x	15	x	40
39	x	14	x	x	x	x	x	x	x	x	x	x	x	x				8						x	x	x	x	x	x	x	x	x	x	x	14	x	39
38																																					38
37																																					37
36																																					36
35																																					35
34			6					x	x	6	x	x	x																					24			34
33			4		x	x	x	x	x	10	x	x	x	x	x																			22			33
32	x			x	x	x	x	x	x	12	x	x	x	x	x	x	x		x	x	5	x	x				10						x	4	x	x	32
31	x	x	x	x	x	x	x	x	x	24	x	x	x	x	x	x	x	x	x	x	x	x	x				6				x	x	x	6	x	x	31
30	x	x	x	x	x	x	x	x	x	25	x	x	x	x	x	x	x	x	x	x	x	x	x	x			4			x	x	x	x	7	x	x	30
29	x	x	x	x	x	x	x	x	x	25	x	x	x	x	x	x	x	x	x	x	x	x	x	x			4				x	x	x	7	x	x	29
28	x	x	x	x	x	x	x	x	x	24	x	x	x	x	x	x	x	x	x	x	x	x	x				6				x	x	x	6	x	x	28
27	x	x	x	x	x	x	x	x	x	23	x	x	x	x	x	x	x	x	x	x	x						8					x	x	5	x	x	27
26																																					26
25																																					25
24																																					24
23																																					23
22			24																					x	x	6	x	x	x					6			22
21			22																				x	x	x	x	10	x	x	x	x			4			21
20	x	x	4	x						10						x	x	5	x	x				x	x	x	12	x	x	x	x	x				x	20
19	x	x	6	x	x					6				x	x	x	x	x	x	x	x	x	x	x	x	x	24	x	x	x	x	x	x	x	x	x	19
18	x	x	7	x	x	x				4			x	x	x	x	x	x	x	x	x	x	x	x	x	x	25	x	x	x	x	x	x	x	x	x	18
17	x	x	7	x	x	x				4			x	x	x	x	x	x	x	x	x	x	x	x	x	x	25	x	x	x	x	x	x	x	x	x	17
16	x	x	6	x	x					6				x	x	x	x	x	x	x	x	x	x	x	x	x	24	x	x	x	x	x	x	x	x	x	16
15	x	x	5	x	x					8				x	x	x	x	x	x	x	x	x	x	x	x	x	23	x	x	x	x	x	x	x	x	x	15
14																																					14
13																																					13
12																																					12
11																																					11
10		15														x	x	6	x	x	x														15		10
9		13												x	x	x	x	10	x	x	x	x	x												13		9
8		5				x	x	5	x	x			x	x	x	x	x	12	x	x	x	x	x	x			x	x	5	x	x				5		8
7			x	x	x	x	x	x	x	x	x	x	x	x	x	x	x	30	x	x	x	x	x	x	x	x	x	x	x	x	x	x	x				7
6			x	x	x	x	x	x	x	x	x	x	x	x	x	x	x	32	x	x	x	x	x	x	x	x	x	x	x	x	x	x	x	x			6
5			x	x	x	x	x	x	x	x	x	x	x	x	x	x	x	32	x	x	x	x	x	x	x	x	x	x	x	x	x	x	x	x			5
4			x	x	x	x	x	x	x	x	x	x	x	x	x	x	x	30	x	x	x	x	x	x	x	x	x	x	x	x	x	x	x				4
3		4		x	x	x	x	x	x	x	x	x	x	x	x	x	x	28	x	x	x	x	x	x	x	x	x	x	x	x	x	x	x	4			3
2																																					2
1																																					1

| | 36 | 35 | 34 | 33 | 32 | 31 | 30 | 29 | 28 | 27 | 26 | 25 | 24 | 23 | 22 | 21 | 20 | 19 | 18 | 17 | 16 | 15 | 14 | 13 | 12 | 11 | 10 | 9 | 8 | 7 | 6 | 5 | 4 | 3 | 2 | 1 |

One-piece blanket

Repeat each row across the blanket as many times as required for the size you are making.

*Rows 1 and 2: St st two rows.
Row 3: K7, p22, k7.
Row 4: P5, k26, p5.
Row 5: K4, p28, k4.
Row 6: P4, k28, p4.
Row 7: K3, p30, k3.
Row 8: P3, k30, p3.
Row 9: K2, p32, k2.
Row 10: P2, k32, p2.
Rows 11 and 12: Rep Rows 9 and 10.
Row 13: K2, p32, k2.
Row 14: P3, k30, p3.
Row 15: K3, p30, k3.
Row 16: P4, k28, p4.
Row 17: K5, p5, k2, p12, k2, p5, k5.
Row 18: P13, k10, p13.
Row 19: K13, p10, k13.
Row 20: P15, k6, p15.
Rows 21 to 26: St st six rows.
Row 27: P11, k14, p11.
Row 28: K13, p10, k13.
Row 29: P14, k8, p14.

Row 30: K14, p8, k14.
Row 31: P15, k6, p15.
Row 32: K15, p6, k15.
Row 33: P16, k4, p16.
Row 34: K16, p4, k16.
Row 35 and 36: Rep Rows 33 and 34.
Row 37: P16, k4, p16.
Row 38: K15, p6, k15.
Row 39: P15, k6, p15.
Row 40: K14, p8, k14.
Row 41: P6, k2, p5, k10, p5, k2, p6.
Row 42: K5, p26, k5.
Row 43: P5, k26, p5.
Row 44: K3, p30, k3.
Rows 45 to 48: St st four rows.**

Individual squares

Cast on 36 sts.

Work from * to **.

Cast (bind) off.

As you continue up from the horizon into the sky above you, the perspective makes these cloud bases seem larger than those down on the horizon. The pattern in this square is similar to the Lower Stormy Clouds pattern, but the cloud shape is extended vertically.

	1	2	3	4	5	6	7	8	9	10	11	12	13	14	15	16	17	18	19	20	21	22	23	24	25	26	27	28	29	30	31	32	33	34	35	36	
48																																					48
47																																					47
46																																					46
45																																					45
44	x	x	x															30																x	x	x	44
43	x	5	x	x	x													26														x	x	x	5	x	43
42	x	5	x	x	x													26														x	x	x	5	x	42
41	x	6	x	x	x	x			x	x	5	x	x					10						x	x	5	x	x			x	x	x	x	6	x	41
40	x	14	x	x	x	x	x	x	x	x	x	x	x	x				8					x	x	x	x	x	x	x	x	x	x	x	x	14	x	40
39	x	15	x	x	x	x	x	x	x	x	x	x	x	x	x			6				x	x	x	x	x	x	x	x	x	x	x	x	x	15	x	39
38	x	15	x	x	x	x	x	x	x	x	x	x	x	x	x			6				x	x	x	x	x	x	x	x	x	x	x	x	x	15	x	38
37	x	16	x	x	x	x	x	x	x	x	x	x	x	x	x	x		4			x	x	x	x	x	x	x	x	x	x	x	x	x	x	16	x	37
36	x	16	x	x	x	x	x	x	x	x	x	x	x	x	x	x		4			x	x	x	x	x	x	x	x	x	x	x	x	x	x	16	x	36
35	x	16	x	x	x	x	x	x	x	x	x	x	x	x	x	x		4			x	x	x	x	x	x	x	x	x	x	x	x	x	x	16	x	35
34	x	16	x	x	x	x	x	x	x	x	x	x	x	x	x	x		4			x	x	x	x	x	x	x	x	x	x	x	x	x	x	16	x	34
33	x	16	x	x	x	x	x	x	x	x	x	x	x	x	x	x		4			x	x	x	x	x	x	x	x	x	x	x	x	x	x	16	x	33
32	x	15	x	x	x	x	x	x	x	x	x	x	x	x	x			6				x	x	x	x	x	x	x	x	x	x	x	x	x	15	x	32
31	x	15	x	x	x	x	x	x	x	x	x	x	x	x	x			6				x	x	x	x	x	x	x	x	x	x	x	x	x	15	x	31
30	x	14	x	x	x	x	x	x	x	x	x	x	x	x				8					x	x	x	x	x	x	x	x	x	x	x	x	14	x	30
29	x	14	x	x	x	x	x	x	x	x	x	x	x	x				8					x	x	x	x	x	x	x	x	x	x	x	x	14	x	29
28	x	13	x	x	x	x	x	x	x	x	x	x	x					10						x	x	x	x	x	x	x	x	x	x	x	13	x	28
27	x	11	x	x	x	x	x	x	x	x	x							14								x	x	x	x	x	x	x	x	x	11	x	27
26																																					26
25																																					25
24																																					24
23																																					23
22																																					22
21																																					21
20		15														x	x	6	x	x	x														15		20
19		13												x	x	x	x	10	x	x	x	x	x												13		19
18		13												x	x	x	x	10	x	x	x	x	x												13		18
17		5				x	x	5	x	x			x	x	x	x	x	12	x	x	x	x	x	x			x	x	5	x	x				5		17
16		4			x	x	x	x	x	x	x	x	x	x	x	x	x	28	x	x	x	x	x	x	x	x	x	x	x	x	x	x			4		16
15				x	x	x	x	x	x	x	x	x	x	x	x	x	x	30	x	x	x	x	x	x	x	x	x	x	x	x	x	x	x				15
14				x	x	x	x	x	x	x	x	x	x	x	x	x	x	30	x	x	x	x	x	x	x	x	x	x	x	x	x	x	x				14
13			x	x	x	x	x	x	x	x	x	x	x	x	x	x	x	32	x	x	x	x	x	x	x	x	x	x	x	x	x	x	x	x			13
12			x	x	x	x	x	x	x	x	x	x	x	x	x	x	x	32	x	x	x	x	x	x	x	x	x	x	x	x	x	x	x	x			12
11			x	x	x	x	x	x	x	x	x	x	x	x	x	x	x	32	x	x	x	x	x	x	x	x	x	x	x	x	x	x	x	x			11
10			x	x	x	x	x	x	x	x	x	x	x	x	x	x	x	32	x	x	x	x	x	x	x	x	x	x	x	x	x	x	x	x			10
9			x	x	x	x	x	x	x	x	x	x	x	x	x	x	x	32	x	x	x	x	x	x	x	x	x	x	x	x	x	x	x	x			9
8				x	x	x	x	x	x	x	x	x	x	x	x	x	x	30	x	x	x	x	x	x	x	x	x	x	x	x	x	x	x				8
7				x	x	x	x	x	x	x	x	x	x	x	x	x	x	30	x	x	x	x	x	x	x	x	x	x	x	x	x	x	x				7
6		4			x	x	x	x	x	x	x	x	x	x	x	x	x	28	x	x	x	x	x	x	x	x	x	x	x	x	x	x			4		6
5		4			x	x	x	x	x	x	x	x	x	x	x	x	x	28	x	x	x	x	x	x	x	x	x	x	x	x	x	x			4		5
4		5				x	x	x	x	x	x	x	x	x	x	x	x	26	x	x	x	x	x	x	x	x	x	x	x	x	x				5		4
3		7						x	x	x	x	x	x	x	x	x	x	22	x	x	x	x	x	x	x	x	x	x	x						7		3
2																																					2
1																																					1
	36	35	34	33	32	31	30	29	28	27	26	25	24	23	22	21	20	19	18	17	16	15	14	13	12	11	10	9	8	7	6	5	4	3	2	1	

For a smaller baby blanket you might want to combine the two stormy cloud patterns into a smaller square, so this square provides you with a ready-to-go combination of the two previous storm cloud patterns.

One-piece blanket

Repeat each row across the blanket as many times as required for the size you are making.

*Rows 1 and 2: St st two rows.
Row 3: K4, p28, k4.
Row 4: P3, k30, p3.
Row 5: K2, p32, k2.
Row 6: P2, k32, p2.
Row 7: K3, p30, k3.
Row 8: P5, k5, p2, k12, p2, k5, p5.
Row 9: K13, p10, k13.
Row 10: P15, k6, p15.
Rows 11 to 14: St st four rows.
Row 15: P14, k8, p14.
Row 16: K15, p6, k15.
Row 17: P16, k4, p16.
Row 18: K16, p4, k16.
Row 19: P15, k6, p15.
Row 20: K6, p2, k5, p10, k5, p2, k6.
Row 21: P5, k26, p5.
Row 22: K3, p30, k3.
Rows 23 to 26: St st four rows.
Row 27: K7, p22, k7.
Row 28: P5, k26, p5.
Row 29: K4, p28, k4.
Row 30: P4, k28, p4.
Row 31: K3, p30, k3.
Row 32: P3, k30, p3.
Row 33: K2, p32, k2.
Row 34: P2, k32, p2.
Row 35 and 36: Rep Rows 33 and 34.
Row 37: K2, p32, k2.
Row 38: P3, k30, p3.
Row 39: K3, p30, k3.
Row 40: P4, k28, p4.
Row 41: K5, p5, k2, p12, k2, p5, k5.
Row 42: P13, k10, p13.
Row 43: K13, p10, k13.
Row 44: P15, k6, p15.
Rows 45 to 48: St st four rows**.

Individual squares

Cast on 36 sts.

Work from * to **.

Cast (bind) off.

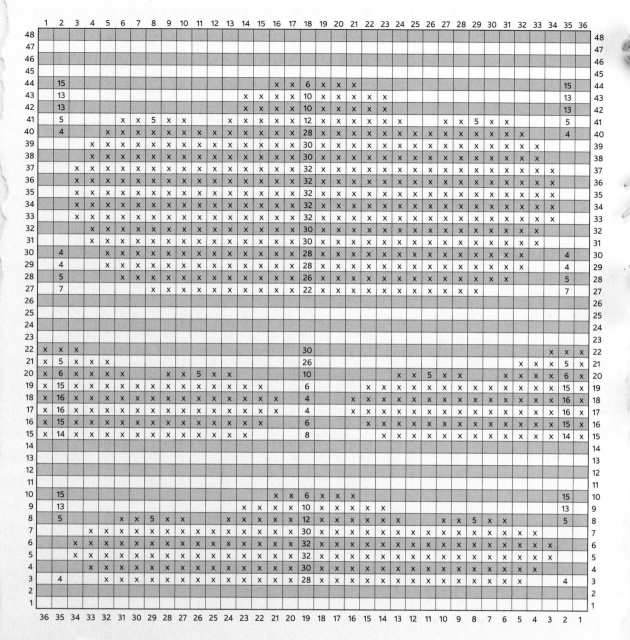

43 /SMALL SUNNY CLOUDS

These are the classic flat-bottomed cumulus cloud shape of many a cartoon sky! As air rises it cools and reaches an elevation where it can't hold all the moisture anymore; this elevation marks the base of the cloud, creating the flat-bottom recreated here with reverse-side stocking (stockinette) stitch.

One-piece blanket

Repeat each row across the blanket as many times as required for the size you are making.

*Rows 1 and 2: St st two rows.
Row 3: K3, p12, k6, p12, k3.
Row 4: P2, k14, p4, k14, p2.
Row 5: K2, p14, k4, p14, k2.
Row 6: P3, k11, p7, k11, p4.
Row 7: K4, p11, k7, p11, k3.
Row 8: P5, k8, p10, k8, p5.
Row 9: K8, p5, k13, p5, k5.
Row 10: P6, k3, p15, k3, p9.
Rows 11 to 14: St st four rows.
Row 15: P8, k6, p12, k6, p4.
Row 16: K5, p4, k14, p4, k9.
Row 17: P9, k4, p14, k4, p5.
Row 18: K3, p7, k11, p7, k8.
Row 19: P8, k7, p11, k7, p3.
Row 20: K2, p10, k8, p10, k6.
Row 21: K1, p5, k13, p5, k12.
Row 22: P13, k3, p15, k3, p2.
Rows 23 to 26: St st four rows.
Row 27: K5, p12, k6, p12, k1.
Row 28: [K14, p4] twice.
Row 29: [K4, p14] twice.
Row 30: P1, k11, p7, k11, p6.
Row 31: K6, p11, k7, p11, k1.
Row 32: P3, k8, p10, k8, p7.
Row 33: K10, p5, k13, p5, k3.
Row 34: P4, k3, p15, k3, p11.
Rows 35 to 38: St st four rows.
Row 39: P6, k6, p12, k6, p6.
Row 40: K7, p4, k14, p4, k7.
Row 41: P7, k4, k14, k4, p7.
Row 42: K5, p7, k11, p7, k6.
Row 43: P6, k7, p11, k7, p5.
Row 44: K4, p10, k8, p10, k4.
Row 45: P4, k13, p5, k13, p1.
Row 46: [P15, k3] twice.
Rows 47 and 48: St st two rows******.

Individual squares

Cast on 36 sts.

Work from * to **.

Cast (bind) off.

Chart (column numbers 1–36 across the top; row numbers 1–48 on both sides; bottom axis numbered 36→1):

Row	1	2	3	4	5	6	7	8	9	10	11	12	13	14	15	16	17	18	19	20	21	22	23	24	25	26	27	28	29	30	31	32	33	34	35	36	Row
48																																					48
47																																					47
46									15							x	x	x							15									x	x	x	46
45	x								13						x	x	5	x	x						13								x	4	x		45
44	x	4	x	x					10						x	x	8	x	x	x	x	x			10								x	x	4	x	44
43	x	5	x	x	x				7				x	x	x	x	11	x	x	x	x	x	x	x			7				x	x	x	x	6	x	43
42	x	5	x	x	x				7				x	x	x	x	11	x	x	x	x	x	x	x			7				x	x	x	x	6	x	42
41	x	7	x	x	x	x	x		4		x	x	x	x	x	x	14	x	x	x	x	x	x	x	x	x	4		x	x	x	x	x	x	7	x	41
40	x	7	x	x	x	x	x		4		x	x	x	x	x	x	14	x	x	x	x	x	x	x	x	x	4		x	x	x	x	x	x	7	x	40
39	x	6	x	x	x	x			6					x	x	x	12	x	x	x	x	x	x				6				x	x	x	x	6	x	39
38																																					38
37																																					37
36																																					36
35																																					35
34		4				x	x	x								15								x	x	x									11		34
33				x	x	5	x	x								13							x	x	5	x	x								10		33
32				x	x	8	x	x	x	x	x					10							x	x	8	x	x	x	x	x					7		32
31		x	x	x	x	11	x	x	x	x	x	x	x			7				x	x	x	x	11	x	x	x	x	x	x					6		31
30		x	x	x	x	11	x	x	x	x	x	x	x			7				x	x	x	x	11	x	x	x	x	x	x					6		30
29	x	x	x	x	x	14	x	x	x	x	x	x	x	x	x	4			x	x	x	x	x	14	x	x	x	x	x	x	x				4		29
28	x	x	x	x	x	14	x	x	x	x	x	x	x	x	x	4			x	x	x	x	x	14	x	x	x	x	x	x	x				4		28
27		x	x	x	x	12	x	x	x	x	x	x	x	x		6				x	x	x	x	12	x	x	x	x	x	x	x				5		27
26																																					26
25																																					25
24																																					24
23																																					23
22						13								x	x	x									15						x	x	x				22
21						12							x	x	5	x	x								13					x	x	5	x	x			21
20	x	x				10							x	x	8	x	x	x	x	x					10					x	x	6	x	x	x	x	20
19	x	x	x			7					x	x	x	x	11	x	x	x	x	x	x	x			7				x	x	x	8	x	x	x	x	19
18	x	x	x			7					x	x	x	x	11	x	x	x	x	x	x	x			7				x	x	x	8	x	x	x	x	18
17	x	5	x	x	x				4				x	x	14	x	x	x	x	x	x	x	x		4				x	x	x	9	x	x	x	x	17
16	x	5	x	x	x				4				x	x	14	x	x	x	x	x	x	x	x		4				x	x	x	9	x	x	x	x	16
15	x	4	x	x					6						12	x	x	x	x	x	x	x			6					x	x	8	x	x	x	x	15
14																																					14
13																																					13
12																																					12
11																																					11
10		6						x	x	x									15						x	x	x								9		10
9		5					x	x	5	x	x								13					x	x	5	x	x							8		9
8		5					x	x	8	x	x	x	x	x					10				x	x	8	x	x	x	x	x					5		8
7				x	x	x	x	11	x	x	x	x	x	x					7				x	x	11	x	x	x	x	x	x				4		7
6				x	x	x	x	11	x	x	x	x	x	x					7				x	x	11	x	x	x	x	x	x				4		6
5			x	x	x	x	x	14	x	x	x	x	x	x	x	x			4				x	x	14	x	x	x	x	x	x	x					5
4			x	x	x	x	x	14	x	x	x	x	x	x	x	x			4				x	x	14	x	x	x	x	x	x	x					4
3				x	x	x	x	12	x	x	x	x	x	x	x				6				x	x	12	x	x	x	x	x	x						3
2																																					2
1																																					1

Bottom axis: 36 35 34 33 32 31 30 29 28 27 26 25 24 23 22 21 20 19 18 17 16 15 14 13 12 11 10 9 8 7 6 5 4 3 2 1

44 /LARGE SUNNY CLOUDS

One-piece blanket

Repeat each row across the blanket as many times as required for the size you are making.

*Rows 1 to 4: St st four rows.
Row 5: K6, p22, k8.
Row 6: P6, k25, p5.
Row 7: K4, p27, k5.
Row 8: P4, k28, p4.
Row 9: K4, p28, k4.
Row 10: P4, k28, p4.
Row 11: K5, p27, k4.
Row 12: P5, k25, p6.
Row 13: K8, p23, k5.
Row 14: P6, k22, p8.
Row 15: K9, p17, k10.
Row 16: P10, k17, p9.
Row 17: K10, p4, k1, p11, k10.
Row 18: P11, k10, p15.
Row 19: K16, p8, k12.
Row 20: P13, k6, p17.
Rows 21 to 28: St st eight rows.
Row 29: P10, k14, p12.
Row 30: K13, p11, k12.
Row 31: P13, k9, p14.
Row 32: K14, p8, k14.

Row 33: P14, k8, p14.
Row 34: K14, p8, k14.
Row 35: P14, k9, p13.
Row 36: K12, p11, k13.
Row 37: P13, k13, p10.
Row 38: K10, p14, k12.
Row 39: P8, k19, p9.
Row 40: K9, p19, k8.
Row 41: P8, k20, p4, k1, p3.
Row 42: K3, p26, k7.
Row 43: P6, k28, p2.
Row 44: K1, p30, k5.
Rows 45 to 48: St st four rows**.

Individual squares

Cast on 36 sts.

Work from * to **.

Cast (bind) off.

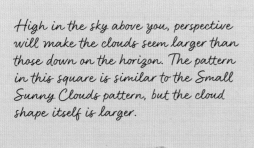

High in the sky above you, perspective will make the clouds seem larger than those down on the horizon. The pattern in this square is similar to the Small Sunny Clouds pattern, but the cloud shape itself is larger.

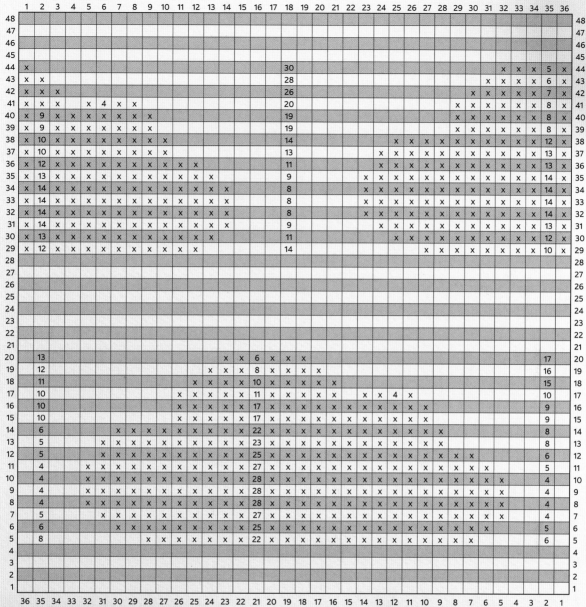

For a smaller baby blanket you might want to combine Small Sunny Clouds and Large Sunny Clouds into a smaller square, so this square provides you with a combination of these two sunny cloud patterns.

One-piece blanket

Repeat each row across the blanket as many times as required for the size you are making.

*Rows 1 and 2: St st two rows.
Row 3: K3, p12, k6, p12, k3.
Row 4: P2, k14, p4, k14, p2.
Row 5: K2, p14, k4, p14, k2.
Row 6: P3, k11, p7, k11, p4.
Row 7: K4, p11, k7, p11, k3.
Row 8: P5, k8, p10, k8, p5.
Row 9: K8, p5, k13, p5, k5.
Row 10: P6, k3, p15, k3, p9.
Rows 11 to 14: St st four rows.
Row 15: P6, k6, p12, k6, p6.
Row 16: K7, p4, k14, p4, k7.
Row 17: P7, k4, p14, k4, p7.
Row 18: K5, p7, k11, p7, k6.
Row 19: P6, k7, p11, k7, p5.
Row 20: K4, p10, k8, p10, k4.
Row 21: P4, k13, p5, k13, p1.
Row 22: [P15, k3] twice.
Rows 23 to 28: St st six rows.
Row 29: K6, p22, k8.
Row 30: P6, k25, p5.
Row 31: K4, p27, k5.

Row 32: P4, k28, p4.
Row 33: K4, p28, k4.
Row 34: P4, k28, p4.
Row 35: K5, p27, k4.
Row 36: P5, k25, p6.
Row 37: K8, p23, k5.
Row 38: P6, k22, p8.
Row 39: K9, p17, k10.
Row 40: P10, k17, p9.
Row 41: K10, p4, k1, p11, k10.
Row 42: P11, k10, p15.
Row 43: K16, p8, k12.
Row 44: P13, k6, p17.
Rows 45 to 48: St st four rows**.

Individual squares

Cast on 36 sts.

Work from * to **.

Cast (bind) off.

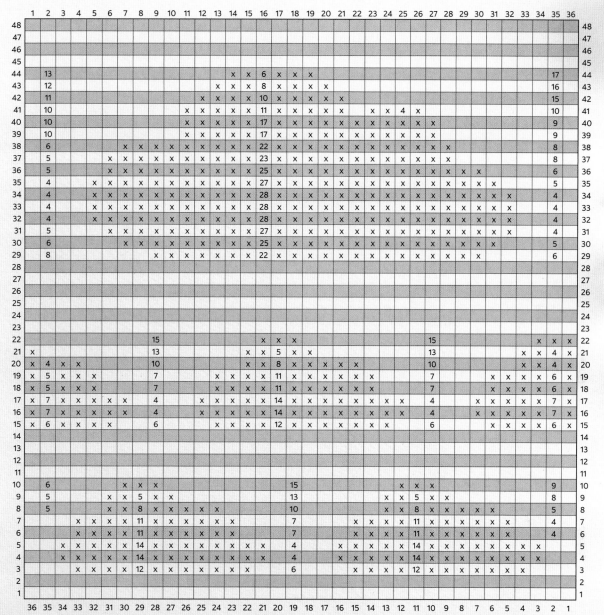

One-piece blanket

Repeat each row across the blanket as many times as required for the size you are making.

*Row 1: K to end.
Row 2: P7, k4, p14, k4, p7.
Row 3: K6, p6, k12, p6, k6.
Row 4: P3, k12, p6, k12, p3.
Row 5: K2, p14, k4, p14, k2.
Row 6: P2, k14, p4, k14, p2.
Row 7: K4, p11, k7, p11, k3.
Row 8: P4, k10, p8, k10, p4.
Row 9: K5, p8, k10, p8, k5.
Row 10: P5, k5, k13, k5, p8.
Row 11: K9, p3, k15, p3, k6.
Rows 12 and 13: St st two rows (starting with a p row).
Row 14: [P14, k4] twice.
Row 15: P5, k12, p6, k12, p1.
Row 16: K4, p6, k12, p6, k8.
Row 17: P9, k4, p14, k4, p5.
Row 18: K5, p4, k14, p4, k9.
Row 19: P8, k7, p11, k7, p3.
Row 20: K3, p8, k10, p8, k7.
Row 21: P6, k10, p8, k10, p2.
Row 22: P12, k5, p13, k5, p1.
Row 23: K2, p3, k15, p3, k13.
Rows 24 and 25: St st two rows (starting with a p row).
Row 26: P5, k4, p14, k4, p9.
Row 27: K8, p6, k12, p6, k4.

Row 28: P1, k12, p6, k12, p5.
Row 29: [K4, p14] twice.
Row 30: [K14, p4] twice.
Row 31: K6, p11, k7, p11, k1.
Row 32: P2, k10, p8, k10, p6.
Row 33: K7, p8, k10, p8, k3.
Row 34: P3, k5, p13, k5, p10.
Row 35: K11, p3, k15, p3, k4.
Rows 36 and 37: St st two rows (starting with a p row).
Row 38: K2, p14, k4, p14, k2.
Row 39: P3, k12, p6, k12, p3.
Row 40: K6, p6, k12, p6, k6.
Row 41: P7, k4, p14, k4, p7.
Row 42: K7, p4, k14, p4, k7.
Row 43: P6, k7, p11, k7, p5.
Row 44: K5, p8, k10, p8, k5.
Row 45: P4, k10, p8, k10, p4.
Row 46: K1, p13, k5, p13, k4.
Row 47: [P3, k15] twice.
Row 48: P to end**.

Individual squares

Cast on 36 sts.

Work from * to **.

Cast (bind) off.

Altocumulus clouds fit together a bit like jigsaw pieces if they have formed from altostratus cloud breaking up. The clouds in this square are based on the Small Sunny Clouds, but are turned into altocumulus clouds by modifying the base to make it less flat, and to make them fit around the other clouds.

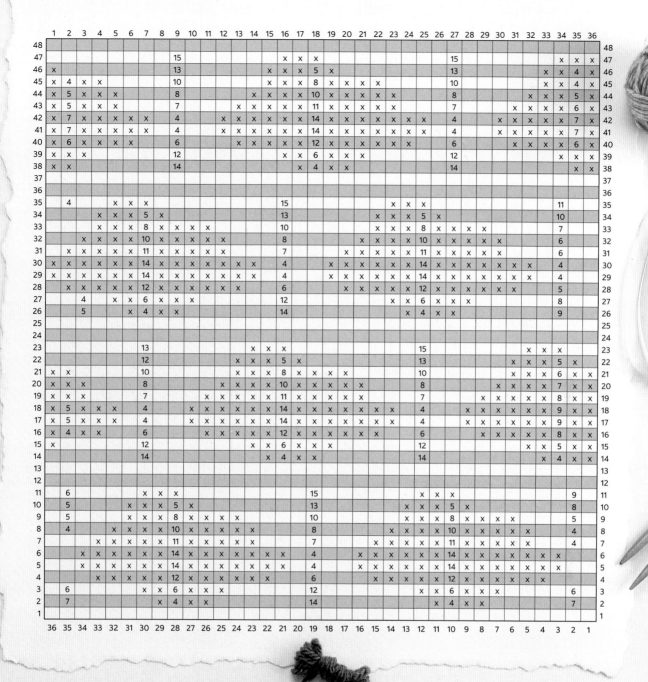

Perspective makes clouds bases that are higher in the sky seem larger than those on the horizon. The pattern in this square is similar to the Small Winter Clouds pattern, but the cloud shape itself is larger.

One-piece blanket

Repeat each row across the blanket as many times as required for the size you are making.

*Rows 1 and 2: St st two rows.
Row 3: K14, p6, k16.
Row 4: P14, k10, p12.
Row 5: K10, p14, k12.
Row 6: P8, k22, p6.
Row 7: K5, p25, k6.
Row 8: P5, k27, p4.
Row 9: K4, p28, k4.
Row 10: P4, k28, p4.
Row 11: K4, p28, k4.
Row 12: P4, k27, p5.
Row 13: K6, p25, k5.
Row 14: P5, k23, p8.
Row 15: K8, p22, k6.
Row 16: P9, k18, p9.
Row 17: K9, p17, k10.
Row 18: P10, k16, p10.
Row 19: K15, p10, k11.
Row 20: P12, k8, p16.
Row 21: K17, p6, k13.
Rows 22 to 26: St st five rows (starting with a p row).
Row 27: P2, k30, p4.
Row 28: K6, p26, k4.
Row 29: P6, k22, p8.
Row 30: K12, p14, k10.
Row 31: P12, k11, p13.
Row 32: K14, p9, k13.

Row 33: P14, k8, p14.
Row 34: K14, p8, k14.
Row 35: P14, k8, k14.
Row 36: K13, p9, k14.
Row 37: P13, k11, p12.
Row 38: K10, p13, k13.
Row 39: P12, k14, p10.
Row 40: K9, p18, k9.
Row 41: P8, k19, p9.
Row 42: K8, p20, k8.
Row 43: P7, k26, p3.
Row 44: K2, p28, k6.
Row 45: P5, k30, p1.
Rows 46 to 48: St st three rows (starting with a p row)**.

Individual squares

Cast on 36 sts.

Work from * to **.

Cast (bind) off.

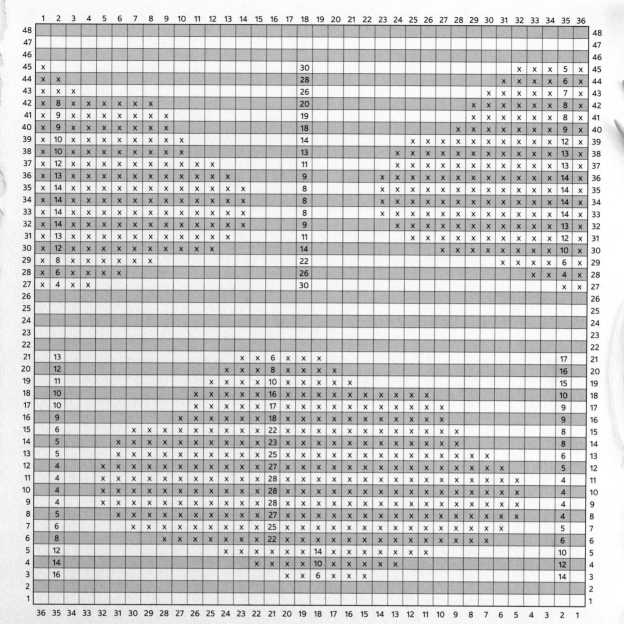

One-piece blanket

Repeat each row across the blanket as many times as required for the size you are making.

*Rows 1 to 6: St st six rows.
Row 7: K13, p8, k15.
Row 8: P13, k12, p11.
Row 9: K10, p14, k12.
Row 10: P11, k16, p9.
Row 11: K8, p18, k10.
Row 12: P7, k24, p5.
Row 13: K4, p27, k5.
Row 14: P4, k29, p3.
Row 15: K2, p30, k4.
Row 16: P3, k31, p2.
Row 17: K2, p32, k2.
Row 18: P2, k32, p2.
Rows 19 to 22: Rep Rows 17 and 18 twice more.
Row 23: K3, p31, k2.
Row 24: P2, k31, p3.
Row 25: K4, p30, k2.
Row 26: P2, k30, p4.
Row 27: K5, p28, k3.
Row 28: P3, k27, p6.
Row 29: K6, p26, k4.

Row 30: P4, k26, p6.
Row 31: K6, p24, k6.
Row 32: P7, k23, p6.
Row 33: K7, p22, k7.
Row 34: P7, k22, p7.
Row 35: K8, p20, k8.
Row 36: P8, k19, p9.
Row 37: K13, p15, k8.
Row 38: P9, k14, p13.
Row 39: K13, p14, k9.
Row 40: P10, k12, p14.
Row 41: K15, p10, k11.
Row 42: P13, k6, p17.
Rows 43 to 48: St st six rows**.

Individual squares

Cast on 36 sts.

Work from * to **.

Cast (bind) off.

The cloud in this pattern could be used with any of the other Sunny and Winter Cloud patterns, because when looking at the flat-bottom of a Sunny Cloud from underneath, it would look more like this pattern.

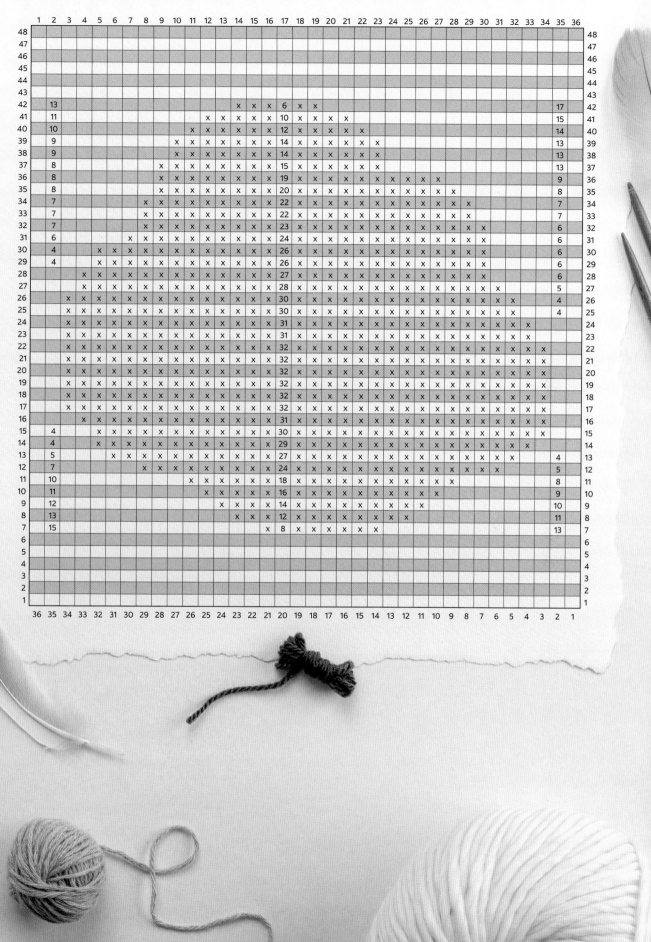

49 / COMBINED WINTER CLOUDS

For a smaller baby blanket you might want to combine two of the winter cloud patterns into a smaller square. This square provides you with a combination of the Small and Medium Winter Clouds. The Large Winter Clouds is too big to combine with other patterns within one square.

One-piece blanket

Repeat each row across the blanket as many times as required for the size you are making.

*Row 1: K to end.
Row 2: P7, k4, p14, k4, p7.
Row 3: K6, p6, k12, p6, k6.
Row 4: P3, k12, p6, k12, p3.
Row 5: K2, p14, k4, p14, k2.
Row 6: P2, k14, p4, k14, p2.
Row 7: K4, p11, k7, p11, k3.
Row 8: P4, k10, p8, k10, p4.
Row 9: K5, p8, k10, p8, k5.
Row 10: P5, k5, p13, k5, p8.
Row 11: K9, p3, k15, p3, k6.
Rows 12 and 13: St st two rows (starting with a p row).
Row 14: K2, p14, k4, p14, k2.
Row 15: P3, k12, p6, k12, p3.
Row 16: K6, p6, k12, p6, k6.
Row 17: P7, k4, p14, k4, p7.
Row 18: K7, p4, k14, p4, k7.
Row 19: P6, k7, p11, k7, p5.
Row 20: K5, p8, k10, p8, k5.
Row 21: P4, k10, p8, k10, p4.
Row 22: K1, p13, k5, p13, k4.
Row 23: [P3, k15] twice.
Rows 24 to 26: St st three rows (starting with a p row).
Row 27: K14, p6, k16.
Row 28: P14, k10, p12.
Row 29: K10, p14, k12.
Row 30: P8, k22, p6.

Row 31: K5, p25, k6.
Row 32: P5, k27, p4.
Row 33: K4, p28, k4.
Row 34: P4, k28, p4.
Row 35: K4, p28, k4.
Row 36: P4, k27, p5.
Row 37: K6, p25, k5.
Row 38: P5, k23, p8.
Row 39: K8, p22, k6.
Row 40: P9, k18, p9.
Row 41: K9, p17, k10.
Row 42: P10, k16, p10.
Row 43: K15, p10, k11.
Row 44: P12, k8, p16.
Row 45: K17, p6, k13.
Rows 46 to 48: St st three rows (starting with a p row)**

Individual squares

Cast on 36 sts.

Work from * to **.

Cast (bind) off.

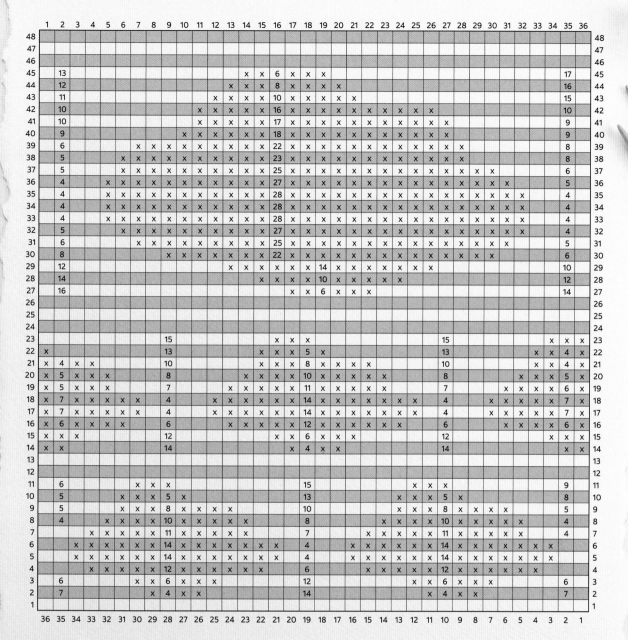

One-piece blanket

Repeat each row across the blanket as many times as required for the size you are making.

*Rows 1 and 2: St st two rows.
Rows 3 to 14: St st 12 rows (starting with a p row).
Row 15: P2, k1, p30, k1, p2.
Row 16: P4, k28, p4.
Row 17: K5, p5, k2, p12, k2, p5, k5.
Row 18: P13, k10, p13.
Row 19: K13, p10, k13.
Row 20: P15, k6, p15.
Row 21 to 26: St st six rows.
Row 27 to 38: St st 12 rows (starting with a p row).
Row 39: P15, k1, p4, k1, p15.
Row 40: K14, p8, k14.

Row 41: P6, k2, p5, k10, p5, k2, p6.
Row 42: K5, p26, k5.
Row 43: P5, k26, p5.
Row 44: K3, p30, k3.
Row 45 to 48: St st four rows**.

Individual squares

Cast on 36 sts.

Work from * to **.

Cast (bind) off.

A looming weather front on the horizon can threaten an incoming rain shower, so this pattern uses the Stormy Cloud patterns as a basis, but joins the individual clouds together to create a characteristic cloud bank. The pattern is repeated to create more interest in an otherwise fairly featureless square.

Knitting/colorwork chart — 36 columns (numbered 1–36 across the top, and 36–1 across the bottom) by 48 rows (numbered 1–48 on both sides).

Numeric stitch-count annotations within the chart:

Row	Annotations (by column)
44	col 18: 30
43	col 2: 5 · col 18: 26 · col 35: 5
42	col 2: 5 · col 18: 26 · col 35: 5
41	col 2: 6 · col 11: 5 · col 18: 10 · col 26: 5 · col 35: 6
40	col 2: 14 · col 18: 8 · col 35: 14
39	col 2: 15 · col 18: 4 · col 35: 15
20	col 3: 15 · col 18: 6 · col 34: 15
19	col 3: 13 · col 18: 10 · col 34: 13
18	col 3: 13 · col 18: 10 · col 34: 13
17	col 3: 5 · col 10: 5 · col 18: 12 · col 27: 5 · col 34: 5
16	col 3: 4 · col 18: 28 · col 34: 4
15	col 18: 30

LOOMING CLOUDS / WEATHER

Blanket
Designs

Sunny Beach

The sun is shining, you have sand between your toes, salt water in your hair and perhaps an ice cream in your hand. The waves lap gently at the shore, you take a deep breath, and for a moment all feels right with the world.

The Sunny Beach blanket demonstrates how a blanket can be made of either individual squares or in one piece – the instructions are given to make the blanket using either construction technique. The yarn used for this pattern is Stylecraft Special DK – the same acrylic yarn used for the swatches in the Pattern Directory.

YOU WILL NEED

Size: 106 x 106cm (41½ x 41½in)

Needles: 3.75mm (US size 5) straight needles and 3.25mm (US size 3) 100cm (40in) circular needle

Yarn: Stylecraft Special DK (light worsted), 100g (3½oz) balls:

- 1 ball of Stone (1710)
- 1 ball of Camel (1420)
- 1 ball of Storm Blue (1722)
- 1 ball of Petrol (1708)
- 1 ball of Aster (1003)
- 1 ball of Lapis (1831)

TENSION (GAUGE): 22 STITCHES X 30 ROWS MEASURE 10Cm (4iN) SQUARE WORKING PLAIN STOCKING STITCH.

Method

To make in squares: Using 3.75mm (US size 5) needles, make individual squares following the patterns shown in the table.

Joining

To make a column of squares as indicated in the table, join the cast on and cast (bound) off edges of each of the square patterns. To join the columns together, match the side seams of each square pattern – making sure to line up the patterns carefully as you go. Use a small offcut of contrasting yarn colour to hold key parts of the pattern in place before you sew the final seam, removing these as you get to them.

Border

Follow the instructions for joining and adding a border in Tips & Techniques: Working a Border, matching the border colours to the squares as required.

Alternative method

To make in one piece with an integral border:

Cast on 226 stitches and work 8 rows of garter stitch.

Knit 5 stitches, place marker, work pattern Row 1 of Many Footprints six times, placing a marker at the end of each repeat, knit 5 stitches.

Continue the above pattern to work the remaining rows of the Many Footprints pattern, slipping markers as you go.

Work the remaining square repeats in the same way, following the table and colours shown.

Work 8 rows of garter stitch.

Cast (bind) off.

Blanket layout

44	44	44	44	44	44
43	43	43	43	43	43
14	14	14	14	14	14
13	13	13	13	13	13
2	2	2	2	2	2
1	1	1	1	2	1

1	MANY FOOTPRINTS, STONE, X 6 SQUARES
2	FEW FOOTPRINTS, CAMEL, X 6 SQUARES
13	LARGE BREAKING WAVES, STORM BLUE, X 6 SQUARES
14	SMALL BREAKING WAVES, PETROL, X 6 SQUARES
43	SMALL SUNNY CLOUDS, ASTER, X 6 SQUARES
44	LARGE SUNNY CLOUDS, LAPIS, X 6 SQUARES

See previous page for an example of this blanket made in one piece.

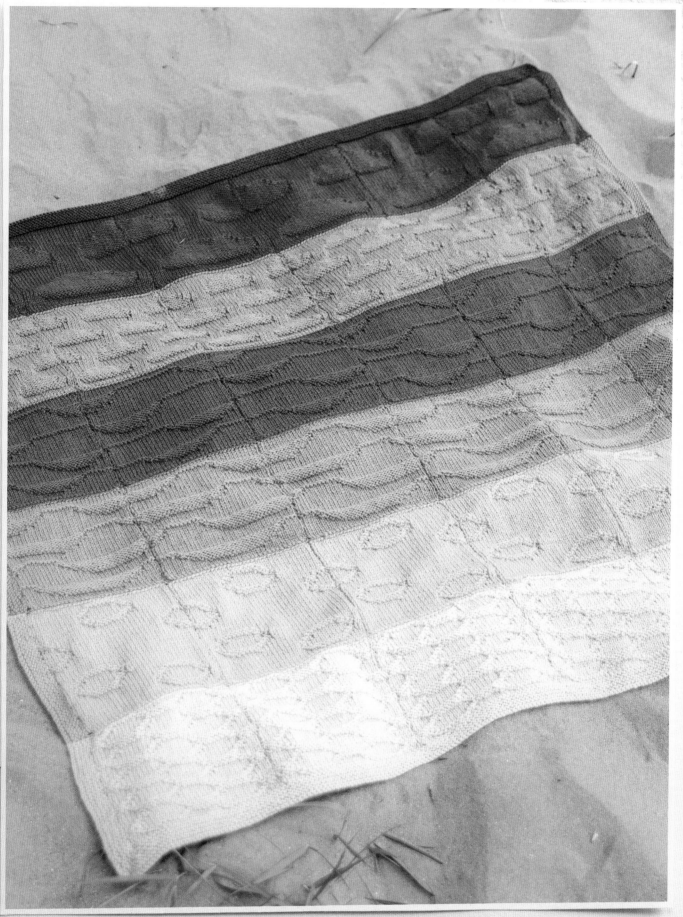

Summer Mountain

Summer in the mountains is such a contrast to the winter, with a range of colours from the greens of conifers, through the colours of the mountains into the blues of the sky. Walking in the mountains in the summer, the cooler temperatures and light breeze, combined with the warmth of the sun, make the world seem fresh and new and full of opportunity!

The Summer Mountain blanket demonstrates how the colour transitions can be softened when making a blanket in distinct rather than gradient colours. Beachscapes tend to have harder horizons, so can suit distinct colour layers. However, for other landscapes, the transition can be softened by using two shades of a similar colour, as shown here. The yarn used in this pattern is Scheepjes Stone Washed, a cotton and acrylic mix, where the colours are softened by the two-tone ply in the yarn. The yarn is labelled Sport but knits up equivalent to DK weight. The tones are light, so they don't obscure the texture; care should be taken when using a multi-coloured yarn, so the colours don't become the feature at the cost of the texture. The blanket is made here from individual squares, but instructions for making in one-piece are also included.

YOU WILL NEED

Size: 106 x 89cm (41½ x 35in)

Needles: 3.75mm (US size 5) straight needles and 3.25mm (US size 3) 100cm (40in) circular needle

Yarn: Scheepjes Stone Washed Sport 50g (1¾oz) balls:

- 2 balls of Malachite (825)
- 2 balls of Fosterite (826)
- 2 balls of Deep Amethyst (811)
- 2 balls of Lilac Quartz (818)
- 2 balls of Turquoise (824)
- 2 balls of Amazonite (813)

TENSION (GAUGE): 22 STS X 30 ROWS MEASURE 10Cm (4in) SQUARE WORKING PLAIN STOCKING STITCH.

Method

To make in squares: Using 3.75mm (US size 5) needles, make individual squares following the patterns shown in the table.

Joining

To make a column of squares as indicated in the table, join the cast on and cast (bound) off edges of each of the square patterns. To join the columns together, match the side seams of each square pattern – making sure to line up the patterns carefully as you go. Use a small offcut of contrasting yarn colour to hold key parts of the pattern in place before you sew the final seam, removing these as you get to them.

Border

Follow the instructions for joining and adding a border in Tips & Techniques: Working a Border, matching the border colours to the squares as required.

Alternative method

To make in one piece with an integral border:

Cast on 190 stitches and work 8 rows of garter stitch.

Knit 5 stitches, place marker, work pattern Row 1 of Large Conifers five times, placing a marker at the end of each repeat, knit 5 stitches.

Continue the above pattern to work the remaining rows of the Large Conifers pattern, slipping the markers as you go.

Work the remaining square repeats in the same way, following the table and colours shown.

Work 8 rows of garter stitch.

Cast (bind) off.

Blanket layout

44	44	44	44	44
43	43	43	43	43
37	37	37	37	37
36	36	36	36	36
34	34	34	34	34
33	33	33	33	33

33	LARGE CONIFERS, MALACHITE, X 5 SQUARES
34	SMALL CONIFERS, FOSTERITE, X 5 SQUARES
36	FOOTHILLS, DEEP AMETHYST, X 5 SQUARES
37	MOUNTAINS, LILAC QUARTZ, X 5 SQUARES
43	SMALL SUNNY CLOUDS, TURQUOISE, X 5 SQUARES
44	LARGE SUNNY CLOUDS, AMAZONITE, X 5 SQUARES

Stormy Beach

It's a stormy day on a sandy beach, with a dark sky looming above and rain falling over the sea. You are wrapped up in waterproofs with the rain pitter-pattering on the hood. The beach is not busy; there are only a few hardy surfers and dog walkers.

The example blanket demonstrated here uses a single yarn cake, a Scheepjes Whirl called "Mid-Morning Mocha'roo", a 4-ply (sportweight) mix of cotton and acrylic. This example is knitted in one piece with a garter stitch border.

If you prefer a sunny beach scene (very sensible), there are other colour options available in the Scheepjes range! You could replace the rain square with the smaller breaking waves, for example.

YOU WILL NEED

Size: 84 x 70cm (33 x 27½in)

Needles: 3mm (US size 2 or 3) 80cm (32in) circular needle

Yarn: Scheepjes Whirl 4-ply (sportweight), 220g (7¾oz) balls:

- 1 ball of Mid-Morning Mocha'roo (766)

TENSION (GAUGE): 26 STS X 35 ROWS MEASURE 10CM (4IN) SQUARE WORKING PLAIN STOCKING STITCH.

Method

Cast on 190 sts and work 8 rows of garter st.

Knit 5 sts, place marker, work pattern Row 1 of Many Footprints five times, placing a marker at the end of each repeat, knit 5 sts.

Continue the above pattern to work the remaining rows of the Many Footprints pattern, slipping the markers as you go.

Work the remaining square repeats in the same way, following the patterns shown in the table.

Work 8 rows of garter st.

Cast (bind) off.

Alternative method

To make in squares: You will not be able to use the yarn cake if you would like to make this blanket from individual squares. Instead choose similar colours for each square pattern row from another yarn. Make individual squares following the patterns shown in the table, then follow the instructions for joining and adding a border in Tips & Techniques: Working a Border, matching the border colours to the squares as required.

Blanket layout

41	41	41	41	41
40	40	40	40	40
39	39	39	39	39
13	13	13	13	13
2	2	2	2	2
1	1	1	1	1

1	MANY FOOTPRINTS X 5 REPEATS
2	FEW FOOTPRINTS X 5 REPEATS
13	LARGE BREAKING WAVES X 5 REPEATS
39	RAIN X 5 REPEATS
40	LOWER STORMY CLOUDS X 5 REPEATS
41	UPPER STORMY CLOUDS X 5 REPEAT

Bluebell Wood

It's a springtime scene for this blanket, with a stream babbling past a carpet of bluebells stretching away beneath the trees. The forest is still a bit damp but starting to dry out with the promise of summer to come. The birds are chirping and somewhere in the distance you hear the sounds of optimistic picnickers enjoying their lunch.

The Bluebell Wood blanket uses another yarn cake from the Scheepjes Whirl range but this time from the Woolly Whirl range, called Kiwi Drizzle, a 4-ply (sportweight) mix of cotton and wool. This example is knitted in one piece with a garter stitch border.

YOU WILL NEED

Size: 80 x 80cm (31½ x 31½in)

Needles: 3mm (US size 2 or 3) 80cm (32in) circular needle

Yarn: Scheepjes Woolly Whirl 4-ply (sportweight), 220g (7¾oz) balls:

- 1 ball of Kiwi Drizzle (473)

TENSION (GAUGE): 26 STS X 35 ROWS MEASURE 10CM (4IN) SQUARE WORKING PLAIN STOCKING STITCH.

Method

Cast on 226 sts and work 8 rows of garter st.

Knit 5 sts, place marker, work pattern Row 1 of Troubled Water six times, placing a marker at the end of each repeat, knit 5 sts.

Continue the above pattern to work the remaining rows of the Troubled Water pattern, slipping the markers as you go.

Work the remaining square repeats in the same way, following the patterns shown in the table. Note that you will need to use the alternative instructions for the two leaf squares to ensure the patterns match at the change of square pattern.

Work Row 1 of Small Beech Leaves once more, then work 7 rows of garter st.

Cast (bind) off.

Alternative method

To make in squares: You will not be able to use the yarn cake if you would like to make this blanket from individual squares. Instead choose similar colours for each square pattern row from another yarn. Make individual squares following the patterns shown in the table, then follow the instructions for joining and adding a border in Tips & Techniques: Working a Border, matching the border colours to the squares as required.

Blanket layout

21	21	21	21	21	21
19	19	19	19	19	19
18	18	18	18	18	18
5	5	5	5	5	5
4	4	4	4	4	4
6	6	6	6	6	6

6	TROUBLED WATER X 6 REPEATS
4	GRASS X 6 REPEATS
5	BLUEBELLS X 6 REPEATS
18	BEECH TREE TRUNKS X 6 REPEATS
19	LARGE BEECH LEAVES X 6 REPEATS
21	SMALL BEECH LEAVES X 6 REPEATS

Deciduous Woodland

The scene is autumnal, with helicopter seeds forming on the maple trees, ready to be dispersed to grow new trees. It has been raining a fair amount, so the well-trodden path has been churned up by many feet.

The Deciduous Woodland blanket shows how 4-ply (sportweight) yarn can be used to create a gradient effect by holding two colours together, and introducing a new colour one at a time. Here, I have used Scheepjes Catona – due to the range of colours available – to create the gradient. The colours shade from the dark brown of muddy footprints through lighter brown tree trunks into green leaves. The brown to green transition is achieved using an olive green where the trunks could be damp and covered in moss. This example blanket is knitted in one piece with a garter stitch border.

YOU WILL NEED

Size: 105 x 95cm (41½ x 37½in)

Needles: 4.5mm (US size 7) 100cm (40in) circular needle

Yarn: Scheepjes Catona 4-ply (sportweight) 50g (1¾oz) balls:

- 2 balls of Black Coffee (162)
- 2 balls of Chocolate (507)
- 2 balls of Hazelnut (503)
- 2 balls of Moon Rock (254)
- 2 balls of Willow (395)
- 2 balls of Sage Green (212)
- 2 balls of Forest Green (412)
- 2 balls of Emerald (515)
- 2 balls of Parrot Green (241)
- 2 balls of Apple Green (389)
- 2 balls of Apple Granny (513)

TENSION (GAUGE): 17 STS X 23 ROWS MEASURE 10CM (4IN) SQUARE WORKING PLAIN STOCKING STITCH.

Method

Using two strands of Black Coffee held together, cast on 154 sts and work 8 rows of garter st.

Break off one strand of Black Coffee and join in one strand of Chocolate. Knit 5 sts, place marker, work pattern Row 1 of Many Footprints four times, placing a marker at the end of each repeat, knit 5 sts.

Continue the above pattern to work Rows 2 to 24 of the Many Footprints pattern, slipping the markers as you go.

Change the remaining strand of Black Coffee to Hazelnut, so you are now working with one strand of Chocolate and one strand of Hazelnut. Continue the above pattern to work Rows 25 to 50 of Many Footprints.

Change the Chocolate strand to Moon Rock. Continue the above pattern to work Rows 1 to 24 of Maple Tree Trunks.

Work the remaining square repeats in the same way, following the patterns shown in the table, changing the strand that you have already used for 48 rows for the next colour in the list of colours shown. Note that you will need to use the alternative instructions for the medium and small leaf squares to ensure the patterns match at the change of square pattern.

Join in the second strand of Apple Granny. With the two strands of Apple Granny held together, work Row 1 of the Small Maple Leaves square once more.

Work 7 rows of garter st.

Cast (bind) off.

Alternative method

To make in squares: Make individual squares following the patterns and colour combinations shown in the table, then follow the instructions for joining and adding a border in Tips & Techniques: Working a Border, matching the border colours to the squares as required.

Blanket layout

25	25	25	25
24	24	24	24
23	23	23	23
22	22	22	22
1	1	1	1

1	MANY FOOTPRINTS X 4 REPEATS, BLACK COFFEE & CHOCOLATE, THEN CHOCOLATE & HAZELNUT
22	MAPLE TREE TRUNKS X 4 REPEATS, HAZELNUT & MOON ROCK, THEN MOON ROCK & WILLOW,
23	LARGE MAPLE LEAVES X 4 REPEATS, WILLOW & SAGE GREEN, THEN SAGE GREEN & FOREST GREEN,
24	MEDIUM MAPLE LEAVES X 4 REPEATS, FOREST GREEN & EMERALD, THEN EMERALD & PARROT GREEN
25	SMALL MAPLE LEAVES X 4 REPEATS, PARROT GREEN & APPLE GREEN, THEN APPLE GREEN & APPLE GRANNY

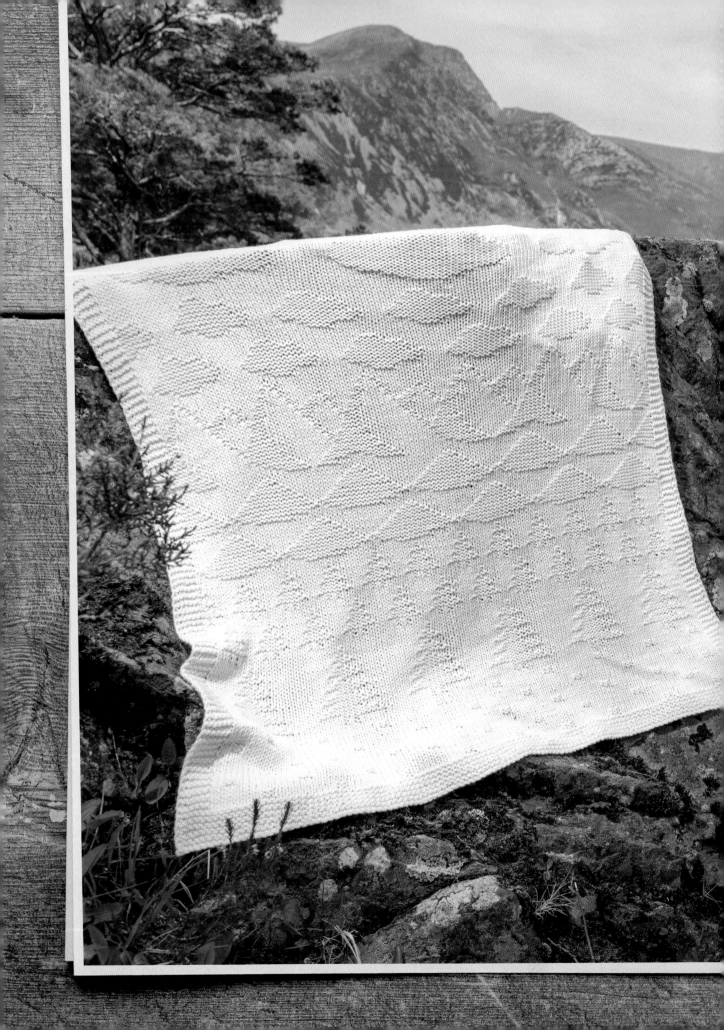

Snowy Mountain

It has snowed heavily overnight and the landscape is covered in a blanket of white. The sky is cloudy, threatening a fresh fall of snow at any moment. You wrap up warm against the cold and go out for a walk. The world is quiet except for the crunch of boots in the fresh snow.

The Snowy Mountain pattern is an example of how the combined squares can be used to create a small baby blanket, whilst still incorporating a range of square patterns. The blanket uses a single colour, here a Sirdar DK (light worsted) bamboo yarn with 80% bamboo and 20% wool, to create a soft blanket suitable for sensitive baby skin. This example is knitted in one piece with a garter stitch border, slipping the first stitch of each row purlwise to create a lacy effect. The yarn is fine for a DK (light worsted) weight, so I have dropped a needle size to help maintain the integrity of the textures.

YOU WILL NEED

Size: 65 x 55cm (25½ x 21½in)

Needles: 3.5mm (US size 4) 80cm (32in) circular needle

Yarn: Sirdar Snuggly Baby Bamboo DK (light worsted), 50g (1¾oz) balls:

- 5 balls of Cream (131)

TENSION (GAUGE): 21 STS X 29 ROWS MEASURE 10Cm (4IN) SQUARE WORKING PLAIN STOCKING STITCH.

Method

Cast on 120 sts.

Slipping the first st of each row purlwise, work 10 rows of garter st.

Slipping the first st purlwise, knit 5 sts, place marker, work pattern Row 1 of Pebbly Sand three times, placing a marker at the end of each repeat, knit 6 sts.

Slipping the first st of each row purlwise, continue the above pattern to work Rows 2 to 24 of the Pebbly Sand pattern, slipping the markers as you go.

Slipping the first st of each row purlwise, continue the above pattern to work all rows of the Combined Conifers pattern, slipping the markers as you go.

Work the remaining square repeats in the same way, following the patterns shown in the table.

Slipping the first st of each row purlwise, work 11 rows of garter st.

Cast (bind) off.

Alternative method

To make in squares: Make individual squares following the patterns shown in the table, then follow the instructions for joining and adding a border in Tips & Techniques: Working a Border, matching the border colours to the squares as required.

Blanket layout

49	49	49
38	38	38
35	35	35
8	8	8

8	PEBBLY SAND X 3 REPEATS
35	COMBINED CONIFERS X 3 REPEATS
38	COMBINED MOUNTAINS X 3 REPEATS
49	COMBINED WINTER CLOUDS X 3 REPEATS

Pebbly Beach

Out for a walk along a pebbly beach in winter, wrapped up warm against the cold, you attempt to keep your balance on deep pebbles. The sky is milky with soft clouds and waves of a grey sea are gently breaking on the pebbles. A dog barks at the sea and children choose pebbles for skimming over the waves.

The Pebbly Beach blanket provides an opportunity for extending your knitting skills; it uses variations of the classic bubble stitch to create different sized pebbles. This blanket, for the pebbles at least, is best knitted as squares, because the pebble patterns have a different number of stitches. A suggestion for how to knit it in a smaller number of pieces is given at the end of the instructions. The blanket is made of recycled yarn, a mixture of 40% wool, 30% acrylic and 30% polyester, giving a new purpose to these recycled fibres. The colours are muted to match the wintery scene. To minimise leftover yarn, the border uses the remaining Smoke yarn, as there is not enough of the Ecru or Sky yarn left. To match the border colour to adjacent squares throughout, you will need another ball of Ecru and Sky.

YOU WILL NEED

Size: 106 x 132cm (41½ x 52in)

Needles: 3.75mm (US size 5) straight needles and 3.25mm (US size 3) 100cm (40in) circular needle

Yarn: Stylecraft Recreate DK (light worsted), 100g (3½oz) balls:

- 2 balls of Ecru (1941)
- 2 balls of Smoke (1943)
- 2 balls of Sky (1946)

TENSION (GAUGE: 22 STS X 30 ROWS MEASURE 10CM (4IN) SQUARE WORKING PLAIN STOCKING STITCH.

Method

To make in squares: Using 3.75mm (US size 5) needles, make individual squares following the patterns shown in the table.

Joining

Block only the non-pebble squares; the pebble squares lose their texture if blocked. I decided the pebbles looked better rotated by 90 degrees, but you can decide what you prefer. If using unrotated pebble squares, join the side seams of each square pattern – making sure to line up the patterns carefully as you go. Use a small offcut of contrasting yarn colour to hold key parts of the pattern in place before you sew the final seam, removing these as you get to them. If using rotated pebble squares, join the cast on and cast (bound) off edges of each square pattern instead.

For the non-pebble squares, join the side seams of each square pattern – making sure to line up the patterns carefully as you go, then join the cast on and cast (bound) off edges of each pattern row, again using marker threads to line up any key joins in the patterns where necessary.

Join the small pebble side seams to the large breaking waves cast on edge.

Border

Follow the border instructions in Tips & Techniques: Working a Border; use Smoke throughout for a single-colour border, or match the colours to the squares for a multi-colour border.

Alternative method

It is a bit tricky to make this blanket in a single piece, but to reduce the joining and finishing time, you can reduce the number of pieces it is made in. I suggest knitting each size pebble as a row or in a column and then joining these together. Once you have the pebble squares as a single piece, pick up 36 stitches per pebble square in Smoke and then knit the waves and sky as a single piece. You can then add a border as per the instructions above.

If you would like to knit this design in one piece, then you will need to decrease the number of stitches you have as you work though the pebble sizes and increase again as you begin the wave patterns.

Blanket layout

48	48	48	48	48	48
47	47	47	47	47	47
46	46	46	46	46	46
14	14	14	14	14	14
13	13	13	13	13	13
12	12	12	12	12	12
11	11	11	11	11	11
10	10	10	10	10	10

10	LARGE PEBBLES, ECRU, X 6 SQUARES
11	MEDIUM PEBBLES, ECRU, X 6 SQUARES
12	SMALL PEBBLES, ECRU, X 6 SQUARES
13	LARGE BREAKING WAVES, SMOKE, X 6 SQUARES
14	SMALL BREAKING WAVES, SMOKE, X 6 SQUARES
46	SMALL WINTER CLOUDS, SKY, X 6 SQUARES
47	MEDIUM WINTER CLOUDS, SKY, X 6 SQUARES
48	LARGE WINTER CLOUDS, SKY, X 6 SQUARES

Tips & Techniques

This section details all the techniques you will need to get started on your blanketscape, including the stitches required, as well as instructions for joining and blocking individual squares if constructed this way. At the end there is also a table of the yarns used in the sample squares.

Abbreviations

cm	centimetres
g	gram
gst	garter stitch
k	knit
k4b	knit 4 below (see Techniques)
k5b	knit 5 below (see Techniques)
k6b	knit 6 below (see Techniques)
mm	millimetres
oz	ounce
p	purl
rep	repeat
RS	right side
st st	stocking (stockinette) stitch
st(s)	stitch(es)
yd	yard
* **	repeat sequence between asterisks
[ ]	repeat sequence in brackets the number of times stated

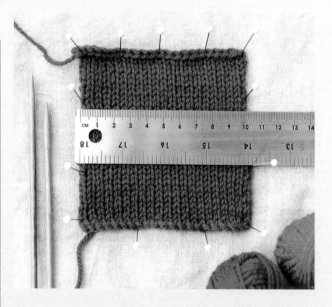

Knitting basics

Tension (gauge)

There is a lot of variation in different yarns, even those that are labelled as being the same weight, so it is always wise to make a tension square before starting work on your blanketscape. To check the tension (gauge) of your knitting, knit a small square of stocking (stockinette) stitch with the stated number of stitches and rows. Lay the knitted square flat and measure the dimensions. If the resulting square is larger than the measurements stated in the pattern, try a smaller needle size. If the resulting square is smaller than the measurements stated, then try a larger needle size.

Casting on

For the first stitch, make a slip knot on the left-hand needle, leaving a long end of yarn for joining if you are making the blanket using individual squares. To make the second stitch, insert the right-hand needle into the first stitch as shown **(A)**. *Wrap the yarn round the right-hand needle from back to front.

Pull the loop through using the right-hand needle, to make a new stitch **(B)**.

Transfer the second stitch to the left-hand needle, taking the left-hand needle up through the stitch from below as shown **(C)**.**

To make the third and remaining stitches, insert the needle through the first and second stitches **(D)**, then repeat from * to ** above to create the new stitch.

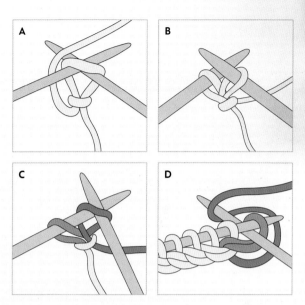

Casting (binding) off

Knit the first two stitches. *Insert the left-hand needle into the first stitch you knitted on the right-hand needle **(E)**.

Pass the first stitch you knitted on the right-hand needle over the second stitch you knitted **(F)**.

Slip the stitch you have passed over off the right-hand needle **(G)**. Knit the next stitch on the left-hand needle so you have two stitches on the right-hand needle once more. Repeat from * to **. When you only have one stitch left, break the yarn – leaving a long end for joining if you are making the blanket from individual squares – and pull the yarn through the stitch until the end.

To cast off purlwise, work the same way as for knitwise but purl the stitches instead of knitting them.

To cast off in pattern, work the same way as for knitwise but work all the stitches as set in the pattern.

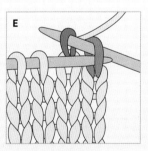

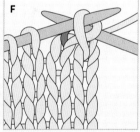

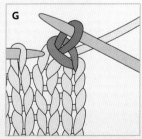

Knit stitch

With the needle with the cast on stitches in your left hand, insert the right-hand needle into the first stitch from front to back as shown **(H)**.

Wrap the yarn round the right-hand needle from back to front **(I)**.

Pull the loop through using the right-hand needle to make a new stitch **(J)**.

Slide the old stitch off the left-hand needle **(K)**.

Purl stitch

With the needle with the cast on stitches in your left hand, insert the right-hand needle into the first stitch from back to front as shown **(L)**, with the left-hand needle in front of the right-hand needle.

Wrap the yarn around the back of the right-hand needle, then back to the front **(M)**.

Pull the loop through using the right-handle needle to make a new stitch **(N)**.

Slide the old stitch off the left-hand needle **(O)**.

Stocking (stockinette) stitch fabric

Stocking stitch is created when you alternate knit and purl rows, to produce the characteristic 'V' shape stitches on the right side of the knitting **(P)**. On the wrong side, you get 'knobbles'; the contrast between the two sides is used to generate most of the textures in this book. The stitches are wider than they are tall, so more rows than stitches are needed to make a square shape. This stitch has a habit of curling at the edges rather than sitting flat, which means a garter stitch border is needed to prevent the squares at the edge of the blanket from curling.

Garter stitch fabric

Garter stitch is created when you knit every row, leading to 'knobbles' on both sides of the knitting **(Q)**. Garter stitch sits flat, so is perfect for a border for the blanket to stop the stocking (stockinette) stitch curling.

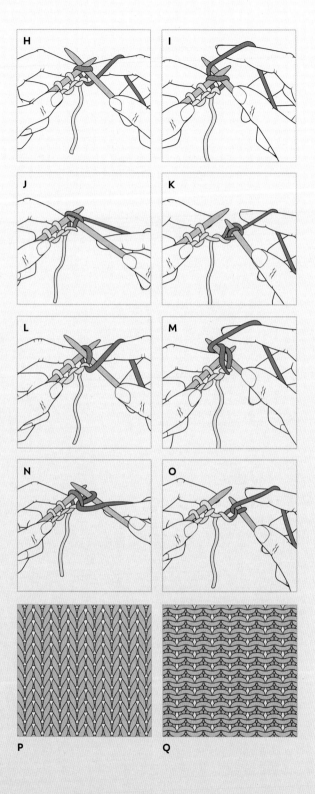

Special stitches

Drop stitch

Slip the stitch to be dropped off the left-hand needle
(A). 'Drop' the stitch down the specified number of rows
(B). Insert the right-hand needle back into the stitch **(C)**.
With the "ladders" in front of the right-hand needle, wrap
the yarn round the right-hand needle from back to front
as you would with a knit stitch **(D)**. Pull the loop through
the dropped stitch to make a new stitch **(E)**.

Slipping a stitch purlwise

Insert the right-hand needle into the stitch on the left-
hand needle, as if you are going to purl the stitch **(F)**. Do
not carry out the rest of the purl stitch – just transfer the
stitch over to the right-hand needle without making a
new stitch.

Pick up and knit

With the right-side facing, insert the left-hand needle
into the knitting where you wish to create a stitch **(G)**.
Pull a loop of yarn through **(H)** and then knit the stitch as
usual on to the right-hand needle. Repeat the stitch as
many times as required.

When picking up stitches on the side edge of stocking
stitch, you need to knit into three stitches, then miss
one, approximately **(I)**, to match the cast on and cast-on
edges.

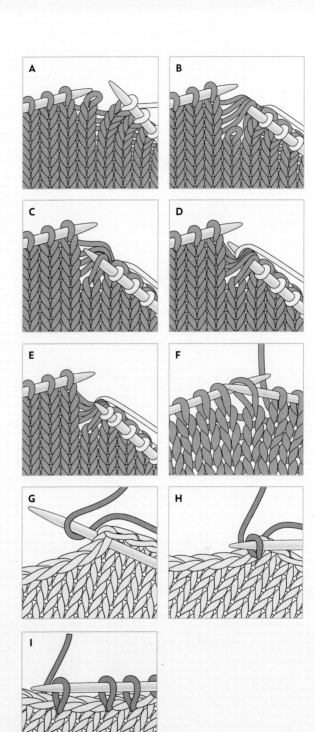

Finishing techniques

Joining

To join two pieces with whip stitch, lay both pieces wrong sides together with the edges to be joined aligned. Thread a length of yarn into a yarn needle. Leaving a long yarn end to be woven in later, oversew the two edges together along the seam **(A)**. Fasten off and then weave in the end at the start.

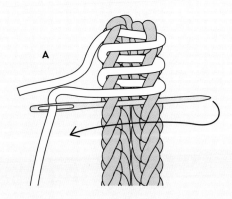

Working a border

When working the border, use a circular needle that is at least one size smaller than those used for the main blanket. For instance, I used a 3.25mm (US size 3) 100cm (40in) circular needle for the border of a blanket made using 3.75mm (US size 5) needles.

Single-colour border: With the right side facing, pick up and knit 36 stitches per square along the lower edge of the blanket in your chosen colour. Work eight further rows of garter stitch, increasing one stitch at each end of each right-side row. Cast (bind) off. Repeat for the upper edge and two side edges. Join the four border corners to finish.

Multi-colour border: Work lower and upper borders as per the single-colour border, using the adjacent square colour. For the side borders (work one at a time): with the right side facing, pick up and knit 36 stitches per square along the side edges of the blanket in each of the colours of the blanket pattern rows, twisting the yarn strands together at each colour join. Work eight further rows of garter stitch in the appropriate colour pattern, increasing one stitch at each end of each right-side row. Cast (bind) off. Join the four border corners to finish.

Blocking

Blocking the squares (or the finished blanket) evens the stitches out and helps to make the squares the right size and shape. Some of the pattern textures make the knitting scrunch up, so this step is an important finishing step. You can block either by soaking the item, or by using a cool / warm item. The type of blocking approach you use depends on the yarn you have made the blanket from, and often the ball band will have pressing instructions for the particular yarn. I like to play it fairly safe, using lukewarm water with some wool wash for all yarn types. Cotton tends to relax after being blocked, so just needs drying flat, whereas acrylic needs a bit more persuasion, so I pin it out to the required size until dry.

Yarn guide

Here I've listed which yarns were used to make the samples shown for each knitted sample for your reference:

Section	Number	Name	Yarn	Colour
Terrain	1	Many Footprints	Stylecraft Special DK	Stone
	2	Few Footprints	Stylecraft Special DK	Camel
	3	Combined Footprints	Stylecraft Special DK	Camel
	4	Grass	Stylecraft Special DK	Kelly Green
	5	Bluebells	Stylecraft Special DK	Bluebell
	6	Troubled Water	Stylecraft Special DK	Storm Blue
Beach	7	Sand Waves	Stylecraft Special DK	Mocha
	8	Pebbly Sand	Stylecraft Special DK	Mocha
	9	Combined Wet Sand	Stylecraft Special DK	Mocha
	10	Large Pebbles	Stylecraft Recreate DK	Ecru
	11	Medium Pebble	Stylecraft Recreate DK	Ecru
	12	Small Pebbles	Stylecraft Recreate DK	Ecru
	13	Large Breaking Waves	Stylecraft Special DK	Storm Blue
	14	Small Breaking Waves	Stylecraft Special DK	Petrol
	15	Combined Breaking Waves	Stylecraft Special DK	Storm Blue
	16	Palm Tree Trunks	Stylecraft Special DK	Walnut
	17	Palm Tree Fronds	Stylecraft Special DK	Green
Forest	18	Beech Tree Trunks	Stylecraft Special DK	Walnut
	19	Large Beech Leaves	Stylecraft Special DK	Green
	20	Medium Beech Leaves	Stylecraft Special DK	Kelly Green
	21	Small Beech Leaves	Stylecraft Special DK	Grass Green
	22	Maple Tree Trunks	Stylecraft Special DK	Walnut
	23	Large Maple Leaves	Stylecraft Special DK	Green
	24	Medium Maple Leaves	Stylecraft Special DK	Kelly Green
	25	Small Maple Leaves	Stylecraft Special DK	Grass Green
	26	Oak Tree Trunks	Stylecraft Special DK	Walnut
	27	Large Oak Leaves	Stylecraft Special DK	Green
	28	Medium Oak Leaves	Stylecraft Special DK	Kelly Green
	29	Small Oak Leaves	Stylecraft Special DK	Grass Green
	30	Small Mixed Leaves	Stylecraft Special DK	Green
	31	Medium Mixed Leaves	Stylecraft Special DK	Kelly Green
	32	Large Mixed Leaves	Stylecraft Special DK	Grass Green
Mountain	33	Large Conifers	Stylecraft Special DK	Green
	34	Small Conifers	Stylecraft Special DK	Kelly Green
	35	Combined Conifers	Stylecraft Special DK	Kelly Green
	36	Foothills	Stylecraft Special DK	Proper Purple
	37	Mountains	Stylecraft Special DK	Wisteria
	38	Combined Mountains	Stylecraft Special DK	Wisteria
Weather	39	Rain	Stylecraft Special DK	Denim
	40	Lower Stormy Clouds	Stylecraft Special DK	Midnight
	41	Upper Stormy Clouds	Stylecraft Special DK	Midnight
	42	Combined Stormy Clouds	Stylecraft Special DK	Midnight
	43	Small Sunny Clouds	Stylecraft Special DK	Aster
	44	Large Sunny Clouds	Stylecraft Special DK	Lapis
	45	Combined Sunny Clouds	Stylecraft Special DK	Aster
	46	Small Winter Clouds	Stylecraft Recreate DK	Sky
	47	Medium Winter Clouds	Stylecraft Recreate DK	Sky
	48	Large Winter Clouds	Stylecraft Recreate DK	Sky
	49	Combined Winter Clouds	Stylecraft Recreate DK	Sky
	50	Looming Clouds	Stylecraft Special DK	Cloud Blue

Serendipitous photo taken of the unsuspecting author by David Hein-Griggs, encapsulating the ethos of the project perfectly – I had no idea the sign was there!

About the Author

Anne is a University Lecturer in Geography and a knitter, combining both in this book through her love of landscapes and understanding of how they form. She gains inspiration from her travels, both in Devon where she lives, as well as further afield. Her travels are often on two wheels, either by bicycle, or on her Triumph Tiger motorcycle named 'Timmy' (after the dog in the Famous Five).

If you are interested in seeing more of Anne's blanket creations and her travels, she can be found on Instagram and Facebook as @blanketscapes, or on www.blanketscapes.com.

Acknowledgements

The seed idea of this book would not have germinated and flowered without the help of many people. Thanks to Emilie for providing untiring company, patience and photographic assistance on blanketscapes-escapades. Isabel for always being ready to provide a sounding board and making honest and helpful suggestions. Anne-Marie for her support and always being available to help me navigate social media. My "Woolliness" group: Alex, Elizabeth, Isabel, Jen, Jo and Sue for their help and encouragement throughout. My colleagues: David, Ewan, Iain, Ian, Jo, Lucy, Nicola, Nina, Sally, Tim, Toby, Tom and Reuben-the-dog for advice, tree-walks, proof-reading and generally humouring me. Maggie (& Ian) for lending me a blanket book which provided some of the inspiration, Andy, Claire (and her Mum!), Duncan, Karen, Katie and Naomi for general encouragement, and to Dedri Uys for giving me courage to embark on this project. Finally, of course, to all my family who have provided love and encouragement throughout.

Thanks to Scheepjes for supplying yarn, and to Wool-on-the-Exe for helping to promote the project.

Index

A DAVID AND CHARLES BOOK
© David and Charles, Ltd 2023

David and Charles is an imprint of David and Charles, Ltd
Suite A, Tourism House, Pynes Hill, Exeter, EX2 5WS

Text and Designs © Anne Le Brocq 2023
Layout © David and Charles, Ltd 2023
Photography and Images © David and Charles, Ltd 2023,
except those listed below

First published in the UK and USA in 2023

ISBN-13: 9781446310052 paperback
ISBN-13: 9781446310069 EPUB
ISBN-13: 9781446310267 PDF

This book has been printed on paper from approved
suppliers and made from pulp from sustainable sources.

Printed in China through Asia Pacific Offset for:
David and Charles, Ltd
Suite A, Tourism House, Pynes Hill, Exeter, EX2 5WS

10 9 8 7 6 5 4 3 2 1

Publishing Director: Ame Verso
Senior Commissioning Editor: Sarah Callard
Managing Editor: Jeni Chown
Editor: Jessica Cropper
Project Editor: Marie Clayton
Head of Design: Anna Wade
Design and Art Direction: Sarah Rowntree
Pre-press Designer: Susan Reansbury
Photography: Jason Jenkins
Production Manager: Beverley Richardson

David and Charles publishes high-quality books on
a wide range of subjects. For more information visit
www.davidandcharles.com.

Share your makes with us on social media using
#dandcbooks and follow us on Facebook and Instagram
by searching for @dandcbooks.

Layout of the digital edition of this book may vary
depending on reader hardware and display settings.

PICTURE CREDITS

17, 18 (bottom) © Unsplash/martenbjork; 18 (middle) © Unsplash/carlosrb; 19, 29, 34 (bottom), 36 (top), 43, 63, 74
(bottom), 99 © Wikimedia Commons; 23 © The Cleveland Museum of Art/Norman O. Stone and Ella A. Stone
Memorial Fund/William Stanley Haseltine; 34 (middle) © Unsplash/philippdeus; 65, 114, 130 © Adobe Stock;
67 © Unsplash/marionb_photography; 68 (bottom) © Unsplash/markusspiske; 71 (top) © Unsplash/annfossa;
72 (bottom) © Unsplash/maksimshutov; 79 © Unsplash/sepoys; 80 (bottom) © Unsplash/jmeguilos; 85 © The
National Gallery of Art/Gift of Louise Mellon in honour of Mr. and Mrs. Paul Mellon/John Constable; 89 © Rawpixel/
Getty/Simon Alexandre Clément Denis; 91 © Pixabay/Martina Bulková; 95 © The National Gallery of Art/Given in
honor of Gaillard F. Ravenel II by his friends/Pierre-Henri de Valenciennes; 103 © Rawpixel/Francis Augustus Lathrop;
104 (bottom) © Unsplash/jeremybishop.